What leaders
The Wellness Journe
and First Place 4 Health

As the leader of this incredibly important ministry, Vicki Heath embodies a powerhouse of possibilities for learning to live a healthy lifestyle. If you need guidance in balancing the ability to thrive on earth while migrating towards a heavenly future, FP4H is a great place to start. I have the utmost admiration and confidence in the leadership and principles held by FP4H. Real help is right here.

Candy Davison, Women's Ministry Coordinator, Sandy Cove Ministries

FP4H has transformed the way I balance the physical, mental, emotional, and spiritual dimensions of my life. National Director Vicki Heath is an extraordinary communicator, motivator, and encourager. She is an energized leader who has helped me set achievable goals and has continued to hold me accountable for making the best choices for good health and balanced living. I highly recommend this program.

Carol Kent, Speaker and Author,
***Becoming a Woman of Influence* (NavPress)**

Vicki Heath has a heart for the health of the body of Christ as no other. Her goals through FP4H are simple: change the Christian, change the church, change the world. With a total-person approach to wellness, FP4H is not just a diet but a lifestyle that works and is sustainable.

Georgia Shaffer, PA Licensed Psychologist and Christian Life Coach, and Author, *Taking Out Your Emotional Trash,*

FP4H helped save my life, my ministry, and my future. The emphasis on becoming balanced and healthy in body, soul, and spirit that First Place 4 Health layers into your life is given to you in a smart, easy to access, and simple-to-live-out ways. My own books teach how God wants us to live longer and stronger, and FP4H made this a consistent lifestyle for me. I will be forever grateful for the results of FP4H in my life, but even more thankful for helping me to become a happier and healthier woman who lives closer to the heartbeat of God.

Pam Farrel, international speaker, author of 40 books including *Men Are Like Waffles, Women Are Like Spaghetti; Devotions for Women on the Go; 10 Best Decisions a Woman Can Make.*

It has been a blessing to work with Vicki Heath for two decades, partnering in ministry to serve those who want to pursue wellness through the FP4H plan, Bible studies, and Body & Soul Fitness classes. Vicki has shown exceptional leadership in both ministries, inspiring women and men to take care of their physical health while also nurturing their spiritual fitness. The FP4H program can be a life-changer for you. I highly recommend that you trust God, jump in, and commit to making it a priority in your life.

Jeannie Blocher, President, Body & Soul Fitness, www.bodyandsoul.org

FP4H helped me lose over 100 pounds and our church lose over 11 tons of weight. My life and our church has been changed forever because of this incredible program. It connects people relationally to become physically, emotionally, mentally, and spiritually healthy. National Director Vicki Heath has a contagious passion for God and wellness that inspires all of us to be our best. She is a transformational leader, speaker, and author. Join the FP4H movement and community.

Steve Reynolds, Pastor, Capital Baptist Church, Annandale, Virginia.

The Wellness Journey
of a
Lifetime

The Wellness Journey
of a
Lifetime

Vicki Heath

First Place 4 Health
7025 W. Tidwell, Suite H-101
Houston, Texas 77092

ISBN #9781942425137

Printed in the U. S. A.

Published by First Place 4 Health,
7025 W. Tidwell, Suite H-101, Houston, Texas 77092.

Published in association with Bold Vision Books,
www.boldvisionbooks.com.

On the cover: FP4H COO, Lisa Lewis

Cover and interior design by kae Creative Solutions.
Editors: Christin Ditchfield, Pat Lewis
Cover photograph by Hunter M. Lewis.

Caution: The information contained in this book is intended to be solely for informational and educational purposes. It is assumed that the First Place 4 Health participant will consult a medical or health professional before beginning this or any other weight loss or physical fitness program.

Information on Bible translations and versions, please see page 159.

Table of Contents

Foreword

Carole Lewis

Vicki Heath is one of the kindest and most generous women I know. Our friendship spans more than twenty years. I have watched Vicki and Rob build a strong marriage, while raising four loving, godly children. Vicki is a stellar pastor's wife, which isn't the easiest job in the world because a pastor and his family live in a fishbowl surrounded by people watching every move.

My first memory of Vicki is when she and Rob brought a group of men, women, and children to Ridgecrest Conference Center in Black Mountain, North Carolina. I was there leading a week-long wellness week for First Place, which Vicki attended with some young people from her local First Place group. As those kids shared stories of how God had used the program to transform their lives and make them stronger, I knew Vicki Heath would be a very special leader in FP4H.

I have watched Vicki go through good times and hard times, and she has never wavered from the woman of God I came to know that week in North Carolina. Vicki will roll up her sleeves and serve in a heartbeat. She is a fabulous cook and has the gift of hospitality as well. I absolutely love to watch her in ministry. She is strong but humble, kind but truthful, patient but persistent to finish the task.

I prayed for two years about when to retire as the director of First Place 4 Health. I knew that God's timing was perfect, and I didn't want to run before Him or lag behind His will. So one day when we had finished the first session of our annual FP4H planning meeting, I was driving home. As has happened before in my life, I was impressed by the Holy Spirit, who lives inside of me, that *now* was perfect for me to retire. I was so excited that I could hardly wait to get out of the car and share the news with the two ladies who were staying with me.

The next morning, I shared my decision to retire with our entire staff. It was December 3, 2013, and the first question was, "when will you retire?" I said, "Let's make it January 1, 2014." I am quite sure that Vicki's emotions that morning were similar to the ones I experienced at Dottie Brewer's funeral in 1989. That day, I felt the true weight of the mantle that had fallen on me.

Foreword ~ Carole Lewis

I'll never forget watching the film of Dottie doing an orientation with her big notebook and posters. I suddenly realized that I was not Dottie and never would be. She taught time management classes and was a type-A personality to the max. Her life was orderly and planned down to the last detail. I, on the other hand, don't know what I will be doing later today—much less a month or year from now.

I believe God called me for the time I served as director of the program, with my unique gifts and skills—plus what He would teach me. Now God has called Vicki with her exceptional ingenuity and talents—and He will teach her everything she needs to know along the way. Vicki is not me and will never be me—but that's a good thing. Vicki has strengths and abilities that I don't have, and she is God's woman to take FP4H to the next level. I am her greatest cheerleader and will love and support her every step of the way.

I am so thankful that God doesn't tell us about all the difficulties we will face in leadership. If He did, none of us would begin—much less complete the task. I believe God has equipped Vicki with everything she needs to lead this wonderful, life-changing program and that He will continue to equip her in the years ahead. Will it be easy? No. Will it be worth it? Absolutely.

The Wellness Journey of a Lifetime

The verses I hung onto during my years of leading FP4H are the same verses I cling to today. They are found in the book of Isaiah.

> I took you from the ends of the earth, from its farthest corners I called you. I said, "You are my servant; I have chosen you. So do not fear, for I am with you; do not be dismayed, for I am your God. I will strengthen you and help you; I will uphold you with my righteous right hand" (Isaiah 41:9-10).

God has chosen Vicki to lead First Place 4 Health, and she will sparkle and shine like only she can. I love our God and I love this woman of God.

Carole Lewis
First Place 4 Health, Director Emeritus

Preface

The Journey

I feel a little like Luke, the Gospel writer, in his opening verse in chapter one. Luke's aim was to recap the Gospel story and give Theophilus the latest update on all that had happened since Jesus came on the scene. Here in this preface, my aim is to give you a written account of the wonderful ministry of First Place 4 Health (FP4H)—how it all got started and what God has done with it ever since. I want to help you discover the impact that God can have in your life when you decide to give Him first place.

The FP4H journey began in 1981, when a group of believers at Houston's First Baptist Church—led by Dottie Brewer—searched for a biblical way to lose weight and develop personal wellness. They believed that God cares about our health and weight, and we must submit every part of our lives to Him for His guidance and direction. First Place 4 Health was originally called First Place. The name came from Matthew 6:33: "Seek ye first the kingdom of God...." These founding folks understood that success in weight loss (as in any other area of life) means Christ must be given first place. They also understood the need for a healthy food plan, so they developed one, along with Bible studies that applied the Word of God directly to weight and health issues.

Encouraged by the initial success of the program, they made First Place materials available to other churches in the Houston area. By 1987, approximately 50 churches had established First Place ministries, and people's lives were changed. Dottie Brewer, founder of First Place, passed the leadership baton to Carole Lewis. Carole describes the day Dottie told her that she was to be the new director:

> "I was flabbergasted because I did not have the organizational skills that Dottie had."

But Carole did have a positive attitude, great public speaking skills, and a real heart for hurting people. She took the ministry of First Place to a new level.

In 1990, LifeWay Christian Resources started publishing all of the First Place program materials, including member resources, books, Bible studies, cookbooks, and journals. They made them available at their bookstores nationwide.

The Journey

It was during this time that I met Carole Lewis. I was leading First Place groups at my church in North Charleston, South Carolina. I took about 20 group members to Ridgecrest Conference Center in Black Mountain, North Carolina, for a week-long First Place wellness program sponsored by LifeWay. I don't recall doing anything special to get noticed, but somehow Carole Lewis spotted me. Carole sees potential in every person she meets.

As a fitness instructor, I set aside special exercise times for my group each morning. Carole noticed. From that week on, she and I became friends. She asked if I would be willing to come, speak, and lead exercise at First Place events. Of course I said, "Yes."

LifeWay's market was predominately Southern Baptist, and First Place wanted to be able to reach more churches in other denominations, so in 1999, the ministry started looking for a new publishing partnership. Gospel Light, in Ventura, California, became our publisher in October of 2000.

In 2006, I officially joined the First Place team, coming on staff to write for the newsletter and to help develop a volunteer leadership base for the ministry. Then in 2004, Gospel Light helped First Place develop a total re-launch of all materials. We updated the program with the latest in nutritional science and all that we had learned, releasing new books, videos, group curriculum, and Bible studies. That's when we became First Place 4 Health. I was involved in creating the new materials, especially the exercise sections. It was my first real attempt at writing. What a big job! But the Lord was with us.

In 2013, big changes came to the ministry. Gospel Light graciously released us from our partnership agreement. We acquired all of the inventory, plus the rights to publish future projects. With all the changes in technology and the publishing industry, we have entered a new paradigm.

At the end of the year, after twenty-four years as the president and public face of the ministry, Carole Lewis announced she was retiring. During her tenure, FP4H had grown from a small group in one church to an international ministry reaching thousands. As a staff, we knew that the day of her retirement would come eventually, but we couldn't really imagine the ministry without her.

Yet she was confident that the Lord had spoken to her the night before, "Carole, this would be a good time for you to retire."

The Journey

Carole's husband, Johnny, battled prostate cancer for years. What God knew—that we didn't—was that He would call Johnny home in the summer of 2014. Since she had retired, Carole was able to spend every minute of that last six months with Johnny.

When Carole left the ministry, she passed the baton to me. On January 1, 2014, I became the national director of First Place 4 Health. I could not be more honored or blessed to be a part of this life-changing ministry. Today as we look to the future, we're more excited than ever about what God will do.

It's a new day, and change is coming. I am praying that as you begin your First Place 4 Health journey, you will find your new paradigm. You must take the first step. Are you ready? Can't you feel it? God is doing a new thing.

> Watch for the new thing I am going to do. It is happening already—you can see it now! I will make a road through the wilderness and give you streams of water there (Isaiah 43:19 GNB).

Vicki Heath
Edisto Island, South Carolina

Acknowledgments

Heroes have poured in time, gifts, and resources to establish First Place 4 Health as the most powerful and effective faith-based weight-loss program in existence. I'd like to thank the following people for their vision and impact on my life and this ministry.

- Carole Lewis, National Director Emeritus, First Place 4 Health, 1987 through 2013, for her energy, perseverance, and genuine heart for people. You are an example of how to do ministry for a lifetime and do it well. Thank you, Carole, for your vision and confidence in me. You have modeled a life of obedience, commitment, and sacrifice.

- The staff at First Place 4 Health, especially Lisa Lewis, for your commitment to the work of the kingdom and for seeing your employment as "more than a job." Your countless hours of work and faithful prayers in support of this ministry are appreciated.

- Current Board of Directors, Karen Porter, Becky Turner, Wendy Lawton, Gari Meacham and Carolyn O'Neal, for your faith and trust in the Lord—and in me—and for teaching me how to lead and how to follow.

The Wellness Journey of a Lifetime

- Regional Team Leaders, Helen Baratta and Delilah Dirksen for years of support, prayers, ideas, accountability, and friendship. You are individually responsible for much of the growth in First Place 4 Health in the last five years.

- All the networking leaders of FP4H for your countless hours and endless miles of volunteering. You are the backbone of our ministry and lives are changed across the country because of you.

- To each leader and member of First Place 4 Health, thank you for the years of loyalty, prayers, and financial contributions you have made to the ministry of First Place 4 Health. I may be unable to thank each of you this day, but there will be a day in eternity. I'm praying for the opportunity in heaven to hug your neck.

- Robin Heath, my husband and pastor, for years of unconditional love.

Introduction

Why Choose FP4H?

With all of the weight-loss programs on the market, why choose First Place 4 Health? Why is this program different? The first and foremost reason is that FP4H is not only about learning a diet or health program, it's about developing a relationship with a person—Jesus Christ. He holds the keys to our success. It is through Him that the power of transformation will come. Other weight-loss plans don't work because they lack His supernatural power. In the last twenty years, dozens of plans have offered tactics, schemes, and diets which promised to slow down the obesity epidemic, but it's only getting worse. America is getting heavier and heavier, and we are paying a price for it.

The data is staggering. The Center for Disease Control gathers information from studies known as the National Health and Nutrition Examination Surveys. These research investigations, which began during the Eisenhower Administration, track the obesity rate periodically.

- Between 1980 and 2000, obesity rates doubled among adults. About 60 million adults, or 30% of the adult population, are now obese.

- Similarly since 1980, overweight rates have doubled among children and tripled among adolescents—increasing the number of years they are exposed to the health risks of obesity.[1]

The United States Department of Agriculture statistics confirm the problem. In the USDA's Agricultural Fact Book, researchers wrote, "According to the National Center for Health Statistics, an astounding 62 percent of adult Americans were overweight in 2000, up from 46 percent in 1980. Twenty-seven percent of adults were so far overweight that they were classified as obese (at least 30 pounds above their healthy weight)—twice the percentage classified as such in 1960.[2]

Obesity is a serious problem.

Some diseases can be prevented or reversed with losing weight—high blood pressure, cardio vascular heart disease, and diabetes to name a few. From 1980 through 2011, the number of Americans with diagnosed diabetes has more than tripled from 5.6 million to 20.9 million.[3]

Why Choose FP4H?

Sleep apnea is another disease that affects many obese people. Can you image getting rid of the sleep apnea machine? Can you imagine never taking high blood pressure medication again? And what if you could enhance your quality of life significantly?

Obesity causes other complications, chronic lower back pain, difficulty maintaining personal hygiene, or gastro-esophageal reflux disease (GERD). FP4H staffer, Helen Baratta, shares how osteoarthritis, particularly in her knees, caused her to pop pain killers simply to be able to stand and do her job. Periodontal gum disease, psychological problems (including social stigmatization and depression), pulmonary hypertension (high blood pressure in the arteries, which carry blood to the lungs), reduced physical mobility, skin problems (including inflammation and infection in skin folds, such as the armpits and the underside of the breasts or belly), and stress-urinary-incontinence are just a few of the other complications caused from obesity. [4]

Today obesity deaths outrank tobacco-related deaths—a staggering statistic.

None of these numbers are any surprise to us. We see the problem everywhere we look—including the mirror!

What is the answer?

The Wellness Journey of a Lifetime

Some believe the problem is financial—so is the solution.

If we only had more money. I always thought if I had enough money, I could whip this weight problem. But the reality is that wealthy real estate moguls, TV personalities, professional athletes—all apparently financially successful—struggle with their weight. According to data by Market Data Enterprises, a market research firm that specializes in tracking niche industries, Americans spend more than $60 billion annually on everything from gym memberships, weight-loss programs, and supplements to diet soda. But the obesity rate has not decreased.

Some think the problem is knowledge—so education must be the answer.

If we only had more education. Surely, if we were better informed about the basic principles of weight loss and the nutritional content of our foods—if we knew exactly how many calories, how much fat, fiber, and sugar they contained—we would be able to make better choices. While I value education, acquiring more information on how to lose weight does not seem to be the answer. There is a huge disconnect between what we know and what we do. Amazon.com currently offers 5,487 books on weight loss. Do we really need more information?

Why Choose FP4H?

I think we need a transformation.

FP4H has a different philosophy—truth. In First Place 4 Health we tell the truth. We teach the truth. We explain how to be changed from the inside out. The wonderful concept found in 2 Corinthians 5:17 "Therefore, if anyone is in Christ, he is a new creature, old things are passed away, and all things become new" (KJV).

Out with the old and in with the new—the spiritual transformation that occurs when God is allowed to make changes from the inside out through the power of the Holy Spirit.

Most weight-loss organizations and programs preach behavior modification, thinking that wellness comes from outwardly changing or controlling unhealthy behaviors. The problem is sustainability. In our own strength, we can modify our actions for a time, but we cannot maintain the changes without a deeper, inner transformation.

In Jesus' day, the Pharisees and experts in the law were convinced that religion consisted of regulating outward behavior. Our culture makes the same mistake. The focus is on keeping rules and regulations, rather than experiencing a genuine change of heart. As a fitness professional, I often hear, "Just tell me what to do." Instead, we *should* be asking, "Tell me how to be."

Our approach to weight loss is backwards. We make our bodies participate in exercises that we don't want to do. We make our bodies "go on a diet" and deprive ourselves of foods we love—foods that are good for us if eaten in the proper portions. Then we hope we will begin to think differently, feel differently about ourselves, and eventually develop a new mindset.

Change Behavior

Change Thinking

Change Mindset

It's a backwards plan, and it does not work. And yet millions have tried to get healthy this way. How many people have decided to get fit, started a diet, exercised like crazy, lost weight, and then gained it all back? The weight lost is temporary, because it's the result of a temporary change in behavior and not a permanent change in thinking.

God's paradigm is the opposite. We first change our mindset, allowing God to have first place in our lives. Then

Why Choose FP4H?

God helps us change our thinking. He transforms us from the inside out, teaching us to replace our old thoughts and attitudes with new, healthier ways of thinking. And only then do we begin to change our behaviors, adding new behaviors that we can walk in for a lifetime. The FP4H approach:

Change Mindset

Change Thinking

Change Behavior

FP4H teaches truth, because truth leads to transformation, and transformation is key. Without it, keeping food journals, exercising every day, and eating good foods will not result in permanent weight loss. In fact, almost 90% of the people who lose weight gain it back and more, because they do not get to the root of the problem.

That's why God wants His truth planted deep within us. Our bodies are His temple. "Do you not know that your bodies are temples of the Holy Spirit, who is in you, whom you have received from God? You are not your own; you were bought at a price. Therefore, honor God with your bodies" (1 Corinthians 6:19-20 NIV). It is my responsibility to keep my temple as clean, pure, and strong as I can. I do not have the right to abuse my body for it is not my own.

Those who are free in Jesus are free indeed. Free

- from worry and fear,
- from discouragement and defeat,
- from perfectionism,
- from the compulsion to think about food all day,
- to look in the mirror again, without self-recrimination,
- to have your picture taken, without dread,
- to actively participate in family activities, and
- to live fully.

Along with the freedom found in Christ, there are other benefits, which you will experience when putting Christ first. Here are a few of the comments posted on our website:

- My marriage was healed.
- I forgave my parents of child abuse.
- I learned to love myself.
- I sought God's forgiveness.
- I came to Christ.
- I got my life back.
- I became an athlete.

Why Choose FP4H?

- God gave me the willpower to eat in moderation.
- I can feel God working on me and in my life almost every minute I live.
- I no longer carry around the burdens of guilt, anger, and frustration.
- My days are filled with thoughts of Him, and I sing praises deep from within me for He rescued me from my own miry pit.

All of these statements were made by people who have experienced FP4H change from the inside out. And I could list many more.

I became friends with Sharolette's mother, Shelby, when my husband and I moved to Edisto Island to pastor Edisto Beach Baptist Church. Sharolette's story will inspire you.

Sharolette Renee Pennington

My name is Sharolette Renee Pennington. I'm 53 years old. I've struggled with my body image since the day I got saved at the age of 10 and the battle began. Satan's job is to kill and destroy. Our battle is flesh versus spirit.

Most of my high school and college years, I was a cheerleader, which helped me keep weight off. Then I joined the United States Air Force, which demanded weight management.

After the death of my father, losing a child and my marriage, I made food my idol. Yes, my idol. I turned to food for comfort, for help, and relief. I'm 5'4" on a small frame. In 2013, I reached (at that time) my all-time high of 201 lbs. The Holy Spirit within me was grieved. My spiritual light was nearly snuffed out. Yet through all of this, I still wanted God's will in my life.

Back in the 1990s, I tried First Place with some success. In 2013, I went to the Internet to find out if it was still available. After calling the 800 number, I reached Vicki Heath. After talking to her for several minutes, I realized that she was the wife of the pastor of my childhood church in Edisto Beach, South Carolina.

Praise God for her spirit of kindness, with no judgment. With her help and encouragement, I went to my pastor and asked for permission to start a class. He had been the pastor of the church for 29 years. He said yes, but warned me not to expect too many to participate and not to get my hopes up. Following Vicki's suggestions, I started the class. Seventeen showed up, and 16 completed the year. Additional classes started as a result, and classes at other churches also came from our humble beginnings. As a whole, our class did great. Lives were changed, deep hurts were healed, and prayers were answered. Weight loss became last on our lists, because we focused on the Bible study and our personal relationships with Christ Jesus.

My little light began to once again shine before others, pointing them to a Christ who saves, heals, and forgives. But then, the Christmas holidays came. So did the pounds. Once again, I felt I had failed.

And I was 207 lbs. This time, I got on my face before the Lord and humbled myself with a broken and contrite heart. I asked Him to please take control of my food choices and to change my desires.

We serve a big God, so I asked for a big solution. The next morning, I woke up and got a glass of water and an apple for breakfast—totally out of character. Always, in the past, I had to force myself to obey, but the Holy Spirit within me helped me to give God control. Each day I asked Him to guide me, and every night I thanked Him.

I've lost 60 pounds, and I'm healthier and happier inside and out than I've ever been. All the praise goes to Jesus Christ. My body is His temple. Today my life centers on what will count for eternity and on Jesus and what I do for Him each day. I've learned that what I eat is a reflection of how I allow Him to care for me. How I look is a reflection of how I love Him.

Start where you are today and ask Him to take control and see the pounds fall off. Remember, Jesus is the source of all blessings, and His accomplishment on the cross is the source of all blessings. We must make the cross of Jesus our focus. With Him all things are possible.

You'll forget me, but if you meet Jesus, you'll never forget Him—and He'll never leave you.

Why Choose FP4H?

Sharolette Renee Pennington

Before

After

First Things First

There is a wonderful story in the Bible in the New Testament Gospel of John. The story takes place on Sunday morning and Mary, friend of Jesus, has gone to the tomb to finish the anointing of His body as part of the Jewish burial process. She finds the tomb empty, but as she is standing there, she hears someone say, "Mary." At that moment, Mary realizes it is Jesus who has called her name. She is able to see Him clearly, and she falls to her knees to worship Him.

The first time I heard Jesus call my name, I did not know who He was. I was about eight-years-old. I had gotten up early on Easter morning and gone outside by myself. It was still dark. I felt an urge to thank God for Easter, even though I didn't understand what it meant. I had a small red New Testament with Psalms, with a gold lantern on the front (I now know it was probably a Gideon New Testament.) It was worn and a bit tattered.

There was one chapter of Scripture that I knew. We learned verses at school in the old days—remember? I found the 23rd Psalm in that tiny Bible, climbed up on the low patio wall, faced east, and read the Psalm out loud to the Lord. It was my first worship experience. I felt the love of God flooding my small child's heart.

A few years later at the age of 18, I heard more when I went to church because a friend invited me. The pastor shared the story of Jesus and of His death and resurrection. He said that anyone wanting to receive Christ as his or her Savior could come forward to pray. I practically ran down the aisle. I knew Jesus was the One I had worshipped all those years before. That was the day my eyes were fully opened. Jesus was waiting for me, and I received Him as my Lord and Savior. He rushed into my life and changed me forever.

On that Sunday, I learned we can't earn our salvation; we are saved by God's grace when we have faith in His Son Jesus Christ. When you understand that you are a sinner and that Christ died for your sins, you ask His forgiveness. Then you turn from your sins—repent. What matters to Him is the attitude of your heart, your honesty. The words you say or pray don't matter that much. Jesus Christ already knows you and loves you. He hears your heart.

I believe He has been calling you. It is not a coincidence that you are reading this book. I knew I was a sinful person, but I did not know how to change until I understood that Jesus' death on the cross was the payment for my sin. I believed with all of my heart that what the Bible says about Jesus is true—that He loved me enough to die for me. I confessed Jesus that day and I confess Him to you today. Not all of us have the same kind of experience, but I must ask you now, my friend, if you have not received Christ as your personal Savior, what is stopping you? Salvation is as simple as ABC. A-Admit you are a sinner, just as I did. B-Believe in your heart that Jesus is the Christ. And C-confess it. You can confess Jesus in a simple prayer to Him, such as the prayer my youth pastor led me to pray:

> *Dear Lord Jesus, I know I am a sinner, and I ask for Your forgiveness. I believe You died for my sins and rose from the dead. I trust and follow You as my Lord and Savior. Guide me and help me to do Your will. In Your name, Amen.*

If you prayed that prayer today, please tell someone. Sharing this good news will be a faith booster, and you will be confessing, just like I did, your newfound faith in Jesus Christ.

The reason this decision is so critical is that the same power that raised Christ from the dead is the power that will bring about the change in your life you long for. This change will not be a temporary change. Jesus wants to lead us in the way everlasting. He will help you lose the weight and keep it off. He will help you in every area of your life. He will help you develop the fruit of the spirit: "love, joy, peace, patience, kindness, goodness, faithfulness, gentleness, self-control" (Galatians 5:22 ESV). God's Spirit will be in control, and you will no longer be out of control. He will help you develop a new way of thinking and a new way of living. He will give you the power to get over past failures and mistakes. He will also help you forgive others who have wronged you, as well as forgive yourself. Some of the first weight He will help you lose is the weight of guilt and shame. Christ in you really is "the hope of glory" (Colossians 1:27). "For nothing is impossible with God" (Luke 1:37).

It all begins when you invite Him in and give Him first place.

Chapter One

The Four-Sided Person

We humans are complex creatures—"fearfully and wonderfully made" (Psalm 139:14) in "the image of God" (Genesis 1:27). We have a tendency in our culture to compartmentalize. If we want to lose weight, we join a gym. When we want to straighten out a relationship, we make an appointment with a counselor. If we want to grow spiritually, we listen to our pastor. If we want to get smarter, we take a course online. This fragmented approach often fails to recognize how all the parts of our personality are connected. Sometimes we need a broader, more comprehensive approach to our problem-solving.

For example, the reason I overeat may not be because I'm hungry. I may be overeating to cope with emotional problems. My anger may be rooted in rejection. My judgmental attitude may be the result of personal frustrations. My obvious physical problems may be obesity or chronic illness

The Four-Sided Person

or aching knees, but the spiritual problem behind it may be disobedience, willfulness, or unforgiveness.

FP4H helps us get to the root of the problem through the four-sided approach found in Mark 12:30.

> Love the Lord your God with all your heart and with all your soul and with all your mind and with all your strength.

When we look at all the ways God wants us to fully love Him—connect with Him and serve Him—we see how everything fits into these four areas mentioned in the verse—physically, spiritually, mentally, and emotionally. These spheres make the four-sided person of FP4H.

How do we find balance in all four areas?

> Seek first His kingdom and His righteousness and all these things will be given to you as well (Matthew 6:33).

Seeking Him first is the secret to living a balanced, healthy life. When we realize that God wants all of us—not only mind or spirit, but body and emotions as well—we will achieve health and wellness in every area.

Monique understands this balanced approach. She realizes that she cannot lose the weight and keep it off without God's help.

Monique Johnson

I was a new Christian when I received a catalog in the mail with an article about First Place 4 Health. Another weight-loss program. But I thought if it was from God, then it couldn't be bad. *Maybe this time, if I had God helping me to lose weight....*

There were no FP4H groups in my area at that time, so if I wanted First Place 4 Health in my church, I had to start a group. I looked at the website to get more information and liked the program. I felt eager to get started and looked forward to helping others—and finally losing weight myself.

I started First Place 4 Health in January 2008. I weighed 183 pounds, my highest weight, which included many pounds gained after being on dozens of different diets. I knew how to lose weight—I was good at it. I lost the weight over and over again, only to gain it back and then some.

With First Place 4 Health came the tools I needed to succeed. In Matthew 6:33, Jesus said, "But seek first His kingdom and His righteousness, and all these things will be given to you as well." Food was my idol—my addiction. The only person who could help me break the addiction was God. I learned how to insert my name in the memory verses referring to love or caring or anything that referred to my relationship with Jesus. For example: "Jesus loves Monique," or "Never will I leave you, Monique." Inserting my name added a personal touch to His promises. They were directed at me and helped me form a relationship with God and get closer to Him.

In my journey to a balanced, healthy lifestyle, the FP4H Bible studies became my hope, and the Word of God encouraged me to keep going when the going got tough. I memorized the weekly Scripture verse. And because I had a verse in my mind, it was then easier to eat healthy and overcome the temptations. I lost 20 pounds.

Then I was at a standstill.

When someone asked me how much weight I had lost or how long it took me, I answered, "This is the first time I have been able to keep the weight off and not smoke." Although that statement was true, it was still an excuse not to go to the next level.

Sometimes we're afraid of success because people might see us differently. I received compliments and attention that I was not sure how to handle.

I learned that I have the opportunity to make the same choices as those of a healthy person.

To get to the next level, I chose to be accountable to my class. I wrote my weight on the whiteboard in our meeting room. If I gained, I wrote the weight in red, even if it was two-tenths of a pound—not to be extra hard on myself but to show how a number so small makes a huge difference. There were times when I knew the number was going to be red, and I didn't want to go to the meeting. It would have been so easy to call someone to take over the class for me. I thought, *If I don't go this week, I will lose the*

weight next week, and then I can write it in black.
We all know what happens when we hide from
the truth. The longer we stay away, the harder it
is to get back on track.

My expectation when I started First Place 4
Health was to lose weight; I thought getting
closer to God would be the bonus. As it turned
out, getting closer to God was the prize, and the
weight loss was the bonus.

God has taken me so far from where I began.
The unpleasant places of my past have become
a small part of my life. God is shaping me into
what I am and what I have yet to become.

I used to be unable to enjoy daily life, because I
did not have peace in my heart. With God's help,
I am able to trust Him to take care of obstacles
I can't control. I still have a long way to go, and
I have to work on balance every day—because
wellness is a journey, it's not something to do
"just for now."

There are areas in my life that still need work.
I asked God to help me overcome them. God
knew we would get confused in the process, so

He gave us a book full of instructions, the Bible, and He gave us the grace to start over each day. Though my life is full of changes, there is one constant. God. He promises to never leave us nor forsake us. God knows everything we have ever done. He sent His Son to the cross so we could have freedom. Our salvation is a gift; we cannot earn it, because our debt has already been paid. Paul explained in Ephesians 2:8, "For it is by grace you have been saved, through faith—and this is not from yourselves, it is the gift of God."

Each day I pray to keep my focus on God. I pray for Him to reveal what I need to do for Him, and I ask Him to help me be responsible for my own actions.

The Four-Sided Person

Monique Johnson

Before

After

Spiritual Fitness—"With All Your Soul"

Learning to love the Lord with all of your soul means setting aside time to develop a relationship with Christ.

The First Place 4 Health spiritual plan includes spending time with the Lord on a daily basis through Bible study, Scripture reading, and prayer.

There's nothing like the written Word of God for showing you the way to salvation through faith in Christ Jesus.

> Every part of Scripture is God-breathed and useful one way or another—showing us truth, exposing our rebellion, correcting our mistakes, training us to live God's way. Through the Word, we are put together and shaped up for the tasks God has for us (2 Timothy 3:16 THE MESSAGE).

Daily Scripture reading highlights the truth of God's Word.

> The words I have spoken to you—they are full of the Spirit and life (John 6:63).

Believe that God will speak to you. Be still and listen. His Word will focus on your deepest feelings during your regular Scripture reading time, and the Holy Spirit will reveal truth to you. His Word will encourage, guide, reveal, and convict. Pay close attention. Learn to know His voice. Helen Baratta discovered the importance of spiritual balance in her wellness journey.

Helen Baratta

I taught myself to smoke cigarettes when my parents divorced. I regret it. I also regret the drugs and alcohol I consumed during my youth. When I finally kicked those bad habits in my 20s, I turned to a new drug—food. The more I ate, the more I hated how I looked. For my wedding, I lost 40 pounds and earned my lifetime Weight Watcher key. After my first pregnancy, I took diet pills. At age 30 when I had my youngest son, my weight gain was even more than before. Once the scale reached more than 200 pounds, it didn't matter how hard I fought or what plan I used, I could not get back to a healthy weight. I am even part of the failed Fen-Phen drug debacle. My picture could appear on a poster for yo-yo dieting.

By 40, I was morbidly obese and living a life far from God. A friend invited me, and continued to invite me, to church. *(Thank you, Jane, for your persistence.)* Finally after two years, I attended her church. When I heard the wonderful news of Jesus, I was all-in and began my new life in Christ.

God loved me, all 270+ pounds. I joined the church. I joined a small group and served with enthusiasm. Though my weight was a problem, I had no hope to lose it, so I did nothing.

The first time I heard about First Place 4 Health, I said, "Not me, I have already tried dieting, and it doesn't work for me." Slowly, God gently nudged me. For more than a year, I searched for God's plan, but I didn't listen to his tender prodding.

In the spring of 2006, while working through a Bible study, I came to the question, "What is God asking you to do that you are not willing to take action on?" Like a sharp arrow the answer pierced me. *I needed to be leading First Place at my church.* Finally, I was willing to hear God loud and clear. I immediately sent an email to my pastor, asking what I needed to do for approval to start First Place at our church. As I told him about the program, he agreed it fit within our church's vision and mission. I ordered the Group Starter Kit and was on my way.

In September 2006, I held my first orientation at our North Fayette campus. I prayed that God would send at least three people. He sent 24. Many in that group were thankful for the program and had been praying for months to have a Christ-centered health program. I was humbled. I stood before the first group at orientation and honestly shared, "I am starting this group because I need it." God removed the lies, and I finally believed there was hope for me. Spiritually, I said "Yes," to the changes I knew the Lord wanted for my life.

As we memorized Scripture, everything changed. Once when the scale got stuck, I discovered my *go-to* verse, "Now what I am commanding you today is not too difficult for you or beyond your reach" (Deuteronomy 30:11).

I recited the verse repeatedly, remembering that losing weight and keeping it off was not too difficult and not beyond my reach. As my heart changed, I pushed past my 50-pound weight loss, then 75, then 100. It took me four years to lose 116 pounds.

Losing weight is one thing. Staying at the healthy weight is an entirely new challenge. Uncovering my emotional eating triggers has been crucial to keep me at a healthy weight. For years, decades, I used food to cope. Food was my comfort, and I retreated to the pantry. I'd open that door and stare—looking for something to eat, whether I was hungry or not.

Now, unless it is a meal or snack time, if I find myself standing at the pantry door, I ask God to show me what stress or anxiety or hassle I am trying to avoid. Most times, He shows me that I am avoiding Him.

I have kept the weight off for years now, and I've discovered that when I make room for God by obeying Him, He provides, redeems, and assists. I encourage you to embrace His change and say yes to all that the Lord has planned.

The Four-Sided Person

Helen Baratta

Before

After

The Wellness Journey of a Lifetime

As we ask God to help us honor Him with our bodies, He helps us choose what to eat, how much to eat, and when to eat—putting into practice the principles of the FP4H program. Positive wellness happens when we make good choices at the grocery store and when we exercise, but the greatest work will be accomplished in those minutes we set aside for quiet time with Him. Our success in keeping all of our other commitments depends on those quiet moments. He may tell you what to eat, how much to eat, and when to eat. God has the perfect food plan for you.

Your First Place 4 Health group will provide you with a Bible study workbook to help you practically apply the truth of God's Word to your life. First Place 4 Health Bible studies are not meant to be complicated, in-depth studies. Rather they are designed to give participants spiritual food for thought in a question-and-answer format that takes about twenty minutes to complete each day. Whether you are a mature Christian or someone just starting a spiritual journey, you will find plenty of inspiration and encouragement. FP4H studies teach biblical concepts and precepts that directly relate to living a God-honoring, healthy lifestyle—with the practical application that so many of us need. As we've said before, more knowledge isn't the answer—it's learning how to apply what we know.

The Four-Sided Person

And this is my prayer; that your love may abound more and more in knowledge and depth of insight, so that you may be able to *discern* what is best and may be pure and blameless until the day of Christ, filled with the fruit of righteousness that comes through Jesus Christ (Philippians1:9-11 *emphasis added*).

Mental Health—"With All Your Mind"

The battle for wellness starts in the mind—a new way of thinking. Many of us grew up with faulty thought patterns, some more toxic than others. *I'm worthless... hopeless... doomed to fail.... It's genetic. It's my metabolism. I'm such a loser.... Everyone I love will leave me, so I might as well leave them first....* These negative thought patterns can hang around for a long time.

One of my thought patterns took years to change. When I was younger, someone told me I should never wear a striped shirt if I did not want to look fat. How ridiculous. I was a small girl. But my entire life, well into adulthood, I avoided stripes of any kind, because this thought pattern had embedded itself in my thinking.

Many of us have believed negative things about our ability to change or exercise self-control or make healthy choices. We believe we will never successfully, permanently lose weight.

We need to have our minds changed.

- Exercise – Is it punishment for my imperfect body?

- Enough – Will I ever know what it means to feel satisfied?

- Ego – Does this make me look fat?

According to 2 Corinthians 10:3, we can "demolish arguments and every pretension that sets itself up against the knowledge of God, and... take captive every thought to make it obedient to Christ." According to this verse, we can learn to separate God's truth from the unhealthy or negative thought patterns we've fallen into or the lies we have believed.

In FP4H, Scripture memory is a key element, empowering us to resist temptation and keep our commitments.

There is nothing more powerful than the Word of God and its ability to change our way of thinking. Some of us have believed the lie that as we age, we lose the ability to memorize. Not true. Everyone can memorize Scripture. Mary Seay is a great example of what can happen if we try.

Mary Seay

Memorizing Scripture was not something I intended to do when I joined my First Place 4 Health class. Even though I came from a Christian home, the only people I knew who quoted Scripture were either preachers or what I considered "religious zealots." The only two verses I could quote were John 3:16 and the shortest verse in the Bible, "Jesus wept" (John 11:35).

There were two women in my FP4H class who would often quote Scripture during our class discussions. It seemed that just at the right moment they could share these "pearls of wisdom" from the Bible, and then tell us where to find it if we wanted to look for ourselves. I realized that being able to quote Scripture gave credence to what the speaker said—it wasn't the speaker's opinion; it was the Word of God.

I had tried to memorize verses before, but my attempts were always short lived. I could recite the verse at class, but a month or even a week later, it was gone. I was convinced that I would never be able to memorize Scripture and shared my fears with my leader.

She refused to accept my excuse and believed in me enough that she offered to help. While we walked together on the treadmills at our church gym, she taught me how to memorize Scripture. She gave me tips on how to remember the reference, and we looked at the verses in the context in which they were written. Each week we added a verse, while practicing the preceding verses. I also listened and sang along to the Scripture memory CD included in the FP4H Bible study. I carried cards with the verses to review while waiting in line or at an appointment. I gave thanks and rejoiced when verses appeared in my head at night and in the morning, because they were becoming a part of me.

And at the end of our twelve-week session, a miracle happened. I was able to say all ten memory verses and give the reference location. No one could ever have made me believe it was possible. But it really happened, and now I am working on my second set of ten verses. Only God! My intention is to keep practicing the old verses, while adding the new.

My motivation for memorizing Scripture is not to win a prize in class or impress anyone with this skill. I will use these verses to defend myself against the lies of our enemy, the devil. Since the beginning of time, the devil has twisted the Word of God to confuse or manipulate us. When Satan asks, "Did God really say..." as in Genesis 3:1, I hope my answer is what Jesus said in the desert: "It is written...." (See Matthew 4:4.)

My deepest desire is for God to make me into the woman He would have me be. But my job is to meet with Him in His Word, to learn what He has in store for me. God proved His love by showing me that I, too, can memorize Holy Scripture and that He will help me do it.

The Wellness Journey of a Lifetime

Mary Seay

The Four-Sided Person

Emotional Health—"With All Your Heart"

The emotional component of FP4H helps us break free from destructive emotional strongholds related to food issues. In addition, we experience the support of others on the same journey

> Greater love has no man than this, that he lay down his life for his friend (John 15:13).

Do you have friends like that? You will find those kinds of friends at FP4H.

The First Place Health 4 life plan for emotional wellness includes a weekly group meeting specifically designed.

- **Combat isolation.** When you come into a First Place 4 Health class, you discover that others are on the same journey. I remember sharing with my group how I used to fantasize about food. They said, "Me too." Who could understand better than those with the same issues? It gave me great freedom to speak about other struggles that I had never shared before.

- **Increase optimism.** When you hear the amazing weight loss stories and testimonies from class members, you will feel encouraged. If it happened for them, it can happen for you. God desires that all of us live a full and abundant life.

- **Provide information.** When my class pointed out that I got off track every day around 3:00 pm, I realized that time of day was when my kids came home from school. My control went out the window, as they came in the door. My class suggested planning a healthy snack ahead of time. FP4H is a great place to discover and share coping techniques.

- **Promote truth.** When you discover how much God loves you, you want to live in obedience. As our group discussed the Scriptures, and I realized how much my bad choices grieved God, I wanted to change.

- **Change self-focus.** When you leave *self* behind and begin to focus on God, your life fills up with meaningful alternatives to eating.

- **Develop friendships.** When we learn to focus on people, instead of food, we develop healthy relationships with one another. FP4H friends are friends for life. No other community of believers is closer and more caring than FP4H folks.

The Four-Sided Person

You are not designed to do life by yourself. Even Jesus surrounded Himself with close friends and a personal support system. The list above is only part of what is accomplished by getting connected and staying connected to your FP4H group.

> Though one may be overpowered, two can defend themselves (Ecclesiastes 4:12).

You will be asked to reach out to other members of your group with intentional acts of encouragement, such as phone calls and emails. Your class will become more than a class; these folks will become family—and life-giving, life-lasting friendships will develop. Together we stand strong.

P. J. Bahr

The Lord has worked in my life since I became involved with First Place 4 Health. One morning at church, the woman in charge of the Bible study program asked if I'd be willing to lead a study at the end of the summer. Never before had anyone asked me to take on anything remotely close to this kind of leadership role. I turned around to see if she was talking to someone behind me.

The Wellness Journey of a Lifetime

Me? No way.

I said I would pray about it, and she said she would pray for me, too.

So in August, our church offered the first FP4H Bible study. After frequent phone calls to my spiritual mentor, I set a start date. Twenty-four people signed up.

On August 15th, our grandson, Andrew, born a few weeks earlier, died of SIDS. I knew it was the enemy attacking me, because I had agreed to lead a Bible study. *Why did I agree to do this? Why did I think FP4H was a class that should be offered at our church?* I was convinced those 24 people didn't need me, and I certainly didn't need them. My distorted thinking told me that if I had not agreed to lead this class, Satan would have left me alone—and my grandson would be alive.

The class was postponed a couple of weeks. On the first night, one woman stood at the back of the room and said, "P. J., how lucky you are that God brought you to us."

I thought, *what kind of a nut is this?*

The Four-Sided Person

She continued, "God obviously knew you were going to be walking through this deep valley, so He brought 24 people to you, in this class, to hold you up in loving prayer."

I was stunned. Humbled. Awed. Grateful. What a beautiful gift she gave me that evening. God turned my darkness into light through the love and support of 24 class members.

> Praise be to the God and Father of our Lord Jesus Christ, the Father of compassion and the God of all comfort, who comforts us in all our troubles, so that we can comfort those in any trouble with the comfort we ourselves receive from God (2 Corinthians 1:3-4).

P. J. Bahr

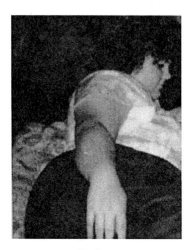

Before

After

The Four-Sided Person

Love, joy, peace, patience, kindness, goodness, faithfulness, gentleness, and self-control. These words are descriptions of emotional wellness, which will be one of the greatest benefits you'll enjoy from learning what it means to give Christ first place.

Finding emotional healing requires the work of self-examination. God, through His Holy Spirit, will lead to the root problem of emotional over-eating. FP4H will provide the tools, but you will do the work—and God will be there every step of the way. Many of us find that our destructive behaviors are connected to experiences or events in our past, which we had no control over—things that were said to us or done to us or the way we were treated by others. But that doesn't mean we are powerless to change.

Jeanne Donovan

The first time I was told that I needed to go on a diet was at the age of seven. As my family gathered around the dinner table, my father turned to me and said, "Girl, you need to go on a diet." I dropped my head in shame, visualizing what a diet would entail. I would be locked away in our small town jail and be fed bread and water until I became slim and trim. Of course, I was never locked away, but my father's cruel words and ridicule were ever-present in the back of my mind. The fat jokes and comments came from others as well, so I hid behind my strong, tough, tomboy self-defense mechanism. Only God and my horse knew the truth, as I shed tears in the dark corner of our barn.

As a college freshman, I chose a career in law enforcement. I had to start exercising a little and lose enough weight to be hired by the California Highway Patrol, and I finally made it. I was out of shape when I reported to the academy. After I endured five grueling months of "boot camp," I graduated—in the best shape of my life. However, this health and vigor didn't last for long.

My career ended after three car accidents, a pursuit, a shooting, a fight, and two back surgeries. In the midst of all of this chaos, I met my wonderful husband, became "mom" to his spry son and lovely daughter, and gave birth to two beautiful girls. I dearly loved my family, but I was fat, miserable, and depressed.

The Four-Sided Person

Over the next 20 years, I tried numerous weight loss programs, but I kept losing and gaining the same 20 pounds. Health issues, along with chronic back pain, slowed my progress. In 2007, the Lord led me in the direction He wanted me to follow. I was in a Christian bookstore and saw a FP4H Bible study and Carole Lewis' book *Divine Diet*. From the moment I began reading and studying, I knew this was what I needed. I did the studies by myself for several years. Then in 2010, a girlfriend from church and a clear urging from God prompted me to start a FP4H group. I enjoy leading my group and encouraging the members to live a balanced life by putting Christ first. My walk with the Lord through FP4H has healed many of my wounds as well and has made my family and me so much healthier.

I should have known, however, that God wasn't through with me yet. In the spring of 2010, Vicki Health asked if I would consider becoming a networking leader for California. I told her I didn't feel I was qualified for that important position, but I would speak with my family, and we would pray about it. My church group was also praying and encouraging me. The Leadership Summit was in July, so I told her we could talk again then. When I arrived in Houston, I was still uncertain, but God knew. He set up divine appointments throughout the weekend for people to pray, encourage, and direct me. As soon as I returned home, I applied for the position. In October 2014, thirty years after my last day with the CHP, I reached two milestones. I was selected to become the networking leader for California, and I achieved my goal weight, having lost 36 pounds. I thank the Lord every day for this new opportunity to serve Him. He has also given me a sisterhood of FP4H friends who have continually prayed for me, as the Holy Spirit knocks down my wall of toughness, and I learn to live for Him.

The Four-Sided Person

Jeanne Donovan

Before

After

Physical Health—"With All Your Strength"

You are living in the only physical body you will ever have on this earth. Taking care of your body is an act of stewardship and a way of honoring God who dwells within us through the Holy Spirit. (See 1 Corinthians 6:19.)

Physical strength is found by

- exercising daily—moving and stretching your body and
- eating well—choosing quality foods in appropriate quantities.

The Lord sanctifies our bodies, as well as our minds and spirits. Sanctification is the process by which we move closer and closer to Christ in this world. Gradually—as we make choices to conform our lives to God's ways—He works in us to help us become a clearer reflection of Christ. We present our bodies to God, because God made us to live full and complete lives. If we allow our natural desires and doubts to rule in our exercise and eating, we run the risk of not allowing God to do His greatest work of sanctification in us—because we've limited His options.

The Four-Sided Person

Our bodies are to be presented like a living sacrifice.

Because God loves us and because of His mercy, we offer ourselves like a sacrifice. Paul wrote, "Therefore, I urge you, brothers, in view of God's mercy, to offer your bodies as living sacrifices, holy and pleasing to God—this is your spiritual act of worship" (Romans 12:1).

Paul called our living sacrifice a spiritual act of worship.

Before the death of Jesus, God's plan included His people offering sacrifices regularly in the temple. Since Jesus paid the penalty for sin on the cross, we no longer need the old sacrifices to make atonement. In essence, we sold ourselves into slavery to sin, but He "purchased us" back with His blood. He bought us so He could free us. And in gratitude, we freely give ourselves back to Him. We present ourselves to God as "living sacrifices." Christ has already made us acceptable in God's sight; now we live in a way that brings glory and honor to Him.

We care for our physical health so that we can not only enjoy the life He's given us, but have the strength and energy we need to accomplish all the things He's called us to do.

According to Scripture God has a plan and a purpose for each one of us. (See Psalm 139 and Jeremiah 29:11.) He's given us gifts and talents that He wants us to use to do the work of His kingdom here on earth. When we make healthy choices, we're choosing to have a heart of worship, choosing to express our gratitude. We're choosing to walk in obedience. Choosing to make ourselves more fully available to Him.

More than Weight Loss

As you can see, the First Place 4 Health program is about much more than weight loss. The First Place 4 Health materials will help you make positive changes in your thought patterns, the way you handle your emotions, the way you fuel and recharge your body with food and exercise, and the way you relate to God and others. The commitments in these four areas—physical, spiritual, mental, emotional—lead to a well-rounded life in Christ.

- Following the exercise and Live-It eating plan will give you a good foundation for physical wellbeing.

- Developing the discipline of a daily quiet time (Bible reading, Scripture memory, and prayer) will nurture your relationship with God and improve your spiritual wellbeing.

- Attending weekly FP4H group meetings will provide the encouragement and support of others, which benefits your emotional wellbeing.

- Establishing a new way of thinking (mental wellbeing) is the key element in the transformation progress.

All of these disciplines have purpose. One purpose is to help us build holy habits, which will lead to freedom. We have all kinds of habits, some good and some not-so-good. But eventually, these actions become ingrained in us—we do them automatically, without thinking. When my son Michael was about ten years old, he was a baseball pitcher. Before every pitch, he reached up and pushed the hair away from his eyes. Even after a haircut, he still did the motion. His habit had become part of his pitching technique.

I want to develop holy habits that are ingrained in my life— such a part of me that I do them automatically. Learning these habits is where First Place 4 Health helps me.

Are you ready to address your issues with each of the four sides—physical, spiritual, mental, and emotional? Are you ready to give God first place and love Him with all your heart, soul, mind, and strength?

If you take the first step, He will meet you and lead you the rest of the way.

Chapter Two

Make Up Your Mind

Many of us have tried and failed to lose weight. And it is hard to think about starting over again. But what have you got to lose if you take a step of faith and give weight loss one more shot with FP4H? You have a lot to lose and a lot to gain.

P. J. Bahr

The first day you join FP4H is the first day of your renewal: mentally, physically, spiritually, and emotionally. Starting today you don't have to live with the same tormenting thoughts you've been waking up with each day: *Why do I have to get out of bed and get dressed today? Nothing's going to fit. I'm too fat for anything I own. I ate so much last night. I dread this.*

Starting tonight, as you lay your head on your pillow to go to sleep, you no longer have to hear the recorded messages in your brain: *I am so horrid. Why did I eat all that today? Oh God, why can't you make me thin like other women? Why do I have to carry this curse around with me all my life?*

You can lay your head on your pillow tonight thanking and praising God that He brought you to First Place 4 Health—the start of something new. With this program, He is going to work *through* you. You don't have to do *anything*, other than be available to Him. By coming to this place, you've let Him know you are willing to step out in faith and be an available vessel through which He will perform a miracle.

Now you can wake up in the morning with a smile and new spirit in your step, knowing that God is with you, at work in you. You will discover a new confidence that "He who began a good work in you will carry it on to completion until the day of Christ Jesus" (Philippians 1:6).

Rather than bemoan, wail, lament, and weep that you are overweight, begin thanking God for your weight. Yes, that's right. Thank Him for the extra weight you carry. Why? Were it not for that "thorn in your side," you might not recognize your need for a Savior or a miracle worker in your life. The Lord used my weight problem to draw me to Him and His miracle-working power. Be happy that you are exactly as you are this day. To God be the glory.

P. J. not only lost weight, she lost her self-loathing attitude, and came to realize her worth in Christ. She grew in confidence that she really could be transformed—she could be made new. She could make healthier choices a part of her lifestyle and lose the weight for good. It started when she made a determined decision to try again.

The impact of a determined decision is wonderfully described in Daniel chapter one. You may recall the story. King Nebuchadnezzar was King of Babylon. He attacked Jerusalem and surrounded the city. The Lord allowed him to capture the temple in Judah, and he took some prisoners back to Babylon.

The king ordered his chief official to select some young men of the royal family from among the Israelite prisoners. The king wanted to recruit them to serve in the royal court so they had to be handsome, intelligent, well-trained, quick to learn, and free from physical defects. Daniel and his friends Hananiah, Mishael, and Azariah, were among those chosen. The king ordered these selected few to be fed the same rich foods, costly meats, and wines as the members of the royal court. It was supposed to be an honor. But for Daniel and his friends, partaking of this food would be a sin—a violation of Jewish dietary laws—because the food had first been sacrificed in worship to false gods. (And we know now that these foods would also have been detrimental to their health.)

Daniel and his friends made up their minds about how to respond. Here are several translations from the Old Testament all from Daniel 1:8 (*emphasis added*):

BBE: "*And Daniel had come to the decision* that he would not make himself unclean with the king's food or wine, so he made a request to the captain of the unsexed servants that he might not make himself unclean."

CEV: "*Daniel made up his mind* to eat and drink only what God had approved for his people to eat. And he asked the king's chief official for permission not to eat the food and wine served in the royal palace."

ESV: "But *Daniel resolved that he would not defile himself* with the king's food, or with the wine that he drank. Therefore, he asked the chief of the eunuchs to allow him not to defile himself."

HCSB: "*Daniel determined* that he would not defile himself with the king's food or with the wine he drank. So he asked permission from the chief official not to defile himself."

KJV: "But *Daniel purposed in his heart* that he would not defile himself with the portion of the king's meat, nor with the wine which he drank: therefore, he requested of the prince of the eunuchs that he might not defile himself."

Each of the translations word it differently, but the message is clear: Daniel made a deliberate, intentional, determined choice to do the right thing. He decided to honor and obey God. And God honored him. Daniel and his friends were allowed to eat the simple fruits and vegetables that met Jewish dietary requirements and had not been offered to idols, and the whole court was amazed by their health and vitality.

Your FP4H journey begins when you make a choice—when you choose to believe that with God's help, you can start again. You decide to commit yourself to honoring Him with your body by making healthy choices (with the help and support of FP4H resources). And you confirm that choice when you make it again every day. Your prayer becomes

> *God, by Your grace, I have made up my mind. I am determined. I am resolved. I purpose in my heart to give You first place....*

Will you make that choice today?

Chapter Three

Get Real

I actually stumbled my way to freedom from an unhealthy relationship with food. I started on my wellness journey with FP4H more than 20 years ago, and I have experienced many victories through the power of Jesus Christ along the way. But I realize now there are also areas I kept hidden. I continued to comfort myself by overeating unhealthy foods. I learned to manipulate the process. I could do the math on the calories and figure out how much exercise it would take to burn off whatever I overate. I was practicing exercise bulimia. I could work a food journal to come out to exactly 1200 calories a day even though I'd made terrible food choices.

FP4H is not a plan to help us manage our sin with tips and tools, but to get to the root of our unhealthy behavior. Until we get to the source of the problem, we will never really get better. We will not lose the weight and keep it off for good. We will continue to wake up every day, and food will consume our thoughts.

We can strive to counteract the consequences of our sin by traditional dieting, but as my friend Gari Meacham says, "Dieting is a carnal way of trying to solve a spiritual problem."

I've struggled with an ungodly relationship with food for many years, always trying to fix it on my own. Several years ago, I finally allowed the Holy Spirit to reveal my problem. One morning during my time of prayer with the Lord, I became quiet and decided to listen to Him. He seemed to ask this question: "What is it that food gives you that I cannot?"

A very good question.

The Holy Spirit convicts of sin and convinces us of our guilt. That day He showed me that I was guilty of three sins:

- The sin of gluttony
- The sin of unbelief
- The sin of idol worship

Get Real

Let's start with gluttony.

Definition: glut·tony *noun*: the act or habit of eating or drinking too much; greedy or excessive indulgence; the view that *gluttony* is a serious failure in self-discipline. First known use of **gluttony**, 13th century. Synonym: overeating. Antonym: abstemiousness.[5]

Not a pretty picture. Gluttony is not a word you hear much. I can count on one finger the number of sermons I have heard preached on this particular sin. But the Bible speaks about gluttony.

> Don't go and stuff yourself! That would be just
> the same as cutting your throat. Don't be greedy
> for all of that fancy food! It may not be so tasty
> (Proverbs 23:3 CEV).

A friend allowed gluttony to destroy her life. She joined my FP4H class several times, only to drop out after a few weeks. She heard the truth from God's Word, but she didn't receive it or believe it. Her obesity started to have serious consequences. Her health was severely impacted, and as her size increased, she lost her mobility. She could barely take care of herself, much less her home and family. Her husband announced he had enough, and she lost her marriage.

Because she couldn't do any chores or housekeeping, her home crumbled around her, and she lost it too. She is still alive—barely. And she is still not willing to give up her unhealthy foods.

It's a cautionary tale, and yet my heart goes out to her. I understand the short-term pleasure that overeating brings. I, too, have participated in the sin of gluttony—consuming more food, out of lust and greed, than anyone person needs. But God has been faithful to forgive me, and that's why I tell my story through FP4H. It's why I do what I do. I want to help others find forgiveness, healing, and freedom—before it's too late.

The second sin God revealed is the sin of unbelief. The reality of unbelief walloped me when I contemplated God's question, "What is it that food gives you that I cannot?"

Every time I give in to food cravings and yield to the flesh, I might as well say,

> *God, I don't believe You. God, you are too weak. God, you are not enough. You are too small, and Your arm is too short. You are too slow. I need something else to satisfy me. You are impotent to help me.*

Get Real

I had many reasons for my abuse of food.

- I couldn't resist. My hand reached out and took the doughnut as if it possessed me.

- I was too tired to cook or make the choice not to eat it.

- I've had a hard day, a hard week, and a hard life.

- I deserve a treat. It's my reward.

God has promised to nourish me. He says He will satisfy me. He tells me life is about a different kind of food than the junk food that so easily tempts me. Jesus said, "Do not work for food that spoils but for food that endures to eternal life, which the Son of Man will give you" (John 6:27).

He also said, "I am the Bread of Life" (John 6:35). Jesus promises to be enough for me. All those years, I had believed more in dinner rolls, than the Bread of Life!

The third sin, which God revealed, is found in one of the most famous stories in the Bible. Moses led Israel out of Egypt after hundreds of years of slavery. They were finally free. Moses went up on Mount Sinai to meet with God, while the people camped down below.

> After the people saw that Moses had been on the mountain for a long time, they went to Aaron and said, "Make us an image of a god who will lead and protect us. Moses brought us out of Egypt, but nobody knows what has happened to him" (Exodus 32:1 CEV).

Why did they build the idol—an image of a calf? Because they were impatient. They would not wait on Moses to come back down. They wondered, *What has happened to him? Maybe he won't come back. Maybe he is dead.*

They didn't believe. Every act of unbelief leads to idol worship.

We begin with a bit of uncertainty, which leads to loss of confidence, and then we find or manufacture another place to put our trust. An idol. We break the first commandment, "You shall have no other gods before me" (Exodus 20:3).

The sin of idol worship is closely related to gluttony. In Paul's letter to the Colossians he warned, "So put to death the sinful, earthly things lurking within you. Have nothing to do with sexual immorality, impurity, lust, and evil desires. Don't be greedy, for a greedy person is an idolater, worshiping the things of this world" (Colossians 3:5 NLT).

Get Real

Gluttony, unbelief, idol worship—three sins in my relationship with food. Food is good, for fuel and comfort (yes, comfort and nourishment), but never for worship.

Food should never have first place.

When I heard Shanda Thornsberry's testimony, I discovered that I was not the only one who had to learn this lesson.

Shanda Thornsberry

Freedom. That's the word that comes to mind when I think of my FP4H testimony. I don't think I grasped the freedom salvation brings until God used FP4H to change my life.

When I was 10 or 11, I raised my hand in Sunday school to say that I wanted Jesus in my heart. But I never grew from that one moment in my faith. I was never mentored, so I did not learn anything about reading my Bible. I *certainly* did not learn about Jesus being my authority. I lived for myself.

I dieted since age 14. I have a family history of obesity, diabetes, heart disease, high blood pressure, and high cholesterol. I was in bondage to food and addicted to sugar. Through God's mercy, I escaped other addictions, but the food addiction was the one I could not master or handle.

As a single adult living alone in my own apartment, I clearly remember going to the grocery store late one night specifically for sugary items. I remember looking into my cart and seeing 9 items—all chocolate and sweets. I can't recall anything I cooked at home regularly as a single, because I ate fast food. And then I carried all those habits into my marriage and packed on 25 more pounds immediately.

In 1999, a couple of years after surrendering my life to the Lord, our church bulletin announced a new class called FP4H—a Christ-centered wellness program. It had never occurred to me to ask for God's help with my weight problem. I promptly joined and met Nancy Smith, my FP4H leader.

Nancy began to teach me *how* to rely on the Spirit in *action*. Through the elements of the program, session after session and year after year, I learned (and continue to learn) how to recognize Jesus as my Lord and authority in the process of surrender and obedience.

The morning God revealed this new idea to me is still clear in my memory. I was determined to have something sweet and had nothing in the house, except brown sugar that I used in baking. I ate some to satisfy my craving, only to go back about every 15 minutes or so until it was completely gone—no small amount. I had attacked the sugar in the same way an addict goes after alcohol or drugs. And I knew I had to face it.

I sat down and had one of the biggest cries of my life, telling the Lord of my sorrow and repentance. I told my husband the truth that morning. I knew I could no longer keep my addiction in the dark, if I wanted to be rescued from it. And I began a new surrender to God, which continues to be a daily decision.

Looking back, I see how I had surrendered to the Lord but had not grown or learned to walk with Him. I had accepted God's free gift of salvation through Jesus and sincerely repented, but I had no idea about the power available to me through the Holy Spirit.

Through my learning process, I tested God—kicking, screaming, complaining, squalling, and digging my heels in—only to find out that God was faithful to me. He equips me, fulfills me, satisfies me, soothes me, comforts me, shows me balance, and empowers me with His Word.

I'm hooked—and I want to keep living this way. Somewhere along the way, I have traded my food addiction for the best craving. And the *only* dependence we're created for—addicted to the One and Only. There's joy unspeakable that accompanies obedience.

I reached a good healthy goal weight in 2010, plus I gained the biggest shift in perspective—when I began to connect my choices to my gratitude for my Savior and view my actions as an act of worship.

Because I love You, Lord, I will put on my tennis shoes and go walk outside with You. Because I love You, Lord, I will enjoy this apple and have a healthy breakfast with You. Because I love You, Lord, I will let You comfort me instead of going into the kitchen right now. I am also honest in my repentance, *I'm sorry, Lord, that I didn't trust You to satisfy me like I thought that candy bar would. Please forgive me that I didn't think You'd be strong enough to soothe me like that dessert.*

It always comes back to what I call the "trusting God" issue. *Do I really believe and trust that God will satisfy me more than this food will?* My prayer is, "help me overcome my unbelief and to know that You, Father, are *big* enough to satisfy me."

The Lord and I have had lots of reconstruction work to do on top of our new foundation—emotional, mental, spiritual, and physical work. I must allow God the time and permission to work in all four areas. My choice is to walk in freedom in God's strength.

Shanda Thornsberry

Before

After

Get Real

Shanda really gets it, and so can you. I repented of my sin, and just like Shanda, I went one step more. I made a point to confess my sin. It is freeing to get it out in the open and admit you need help.

> If we confess our sins he is faithful and just to forgive us our sins and to cleanse us from all unrighteousness (1 John 1:9).

Sins thrive and wounds fester in secrecy.

Why do we keep our sin hidden? Why are we so afraid? God does not want to hurt us. He wants to heal us. "We cannot be healed from that which we keep hidden." I heard Brennan Manning speak those words at a pastors' conference years ago, and the words made a strong impression on me.

I made my confession to God, my group, and my family and friends, but what really sealed my commitment not to participate in these sins any more was an event—an Episcopal women's retreat. I was there speaking on health and wellness. The retreat theme was confession and repentance. At the end of the retreat, participants were asked to take time for personal confession. I confessed publically, telling those ladies that I participated in the sins of gluttony, unbelief, and idol worship. At that moment, those sins lost some of their power over me. Confession really is good for the soul (always to God first). There's such relief in being honest, letting go of the guilt and shame and hypocrisy. For me, that day was part of the healing process.

> Therefore confess your sins to each other and pray for each other so that you may be healed. The prayer of a righteous man is powerful and effective (James 5:16).

We're all on a journey, and it's a process. It takes time. Sometimes victory comes in steps and stages. Until then, we have to do the best we can wherever we are. We continue to seek God for His deliverance and hold up our hearts to the light of His truth.

Food is not the problem; I am the problem. Sin, especially hidden sin, is the problem.

I can now pray, "Lord, thank You for this food and bless it to nourish my body," instead of "Lord, forgive me for what I am about to do." What a joy!

Chapter Four

Food Is Not the Enemy

A young woman asked me to pray that God would help her find a new Bible study group. She quit the group she'd been in, because of the food they served. She had been working hard trying to lose weight and was annoyed because their events seemed to be centered around food. She had shared her weight loss goals with the group and asked them not to serve the food. But they refused. They said, "If you don't want the food, don't eat the food." Or, "Just eat a little."

Frustrated by their lack of consideration—and worried about losing the progress she had made—she'd decided to find another Bible study group less "obsessed" with food.

I questioned, "Is food *really* the problem? Do they gather to talk about and study and worship the food? Do they focus solely on the food?"

She responded, "Well, no. We study the Bible. The food is served at the fellowship time, before we start."

In general, it is a good strategy to avoid situations that could cause us to stumble. But food is everywhere, and we cannot avoid it. A better strategy is to address the deeper issues.

In First Place 4 Heath, we believe that food is rarely the problem. There are many biblical accounts of God blessing food as a part of fellowship. It plays an import role in bringing people together, in feasts, festivals, community, and family celebrations. We gather around the table and give thanks to God. We share our hearts and our food with one another. Furthermore, God commands us to show hospitality. He even gives some people a special gift for it. A big part of hospitality is caring for one another's needs, including the need for physical nourishment. We should be free to enjoy the gifts of fellowship, community, and hospitality—regardless what food is on the table.

Earlier, we talked about how sinful (and unhealthy) it is to allow food to control us through gluttony and idolatry. It's also unhealthy (and sinful) to allow fear of food to control us. I've seen up close how all-consuming that fear can be.

My friend had suffered with anorexia and bulimia her entire life and now battled esophageal cancer. In the last days of her battle, she was not able to swallow any solid food and was starving to death. The doctors placed a stint in her esophagus to widen the opening, so soft foods and liquids could pass through. One day apparently something had become lodged near the stint. I took her to the doctor, and they put her to sleep to run the scope down her throat. They removed a small grain of rice. When she came to, the nurse offered her something to drink.

"What do you have?" she asked.

"Honey, you can have anything you want: Coke, tea, juice, you name it."

"Do you have anything diet? I don't need all that sugar."

I could not believe her words. Although she lay dying, she was still afraid to drink anything that had calories. The fear of being fat still consumed her. A few weeks later, the Lord took my friend home to be with Him. She is now free. But I think of others who still struggle with anxiety over what they "can" and "can't" eat.

At First Place 4 Health, we want you to recognize your food fears and conquer them once and for all. We teach that God intends food for fuel *and* for enjoyment—but never for worship. Food is not meant to be a hobby. It is not your friend. It is not your family. No matter how much you love it, food cannot love you back. You can be free to develop a healthy relationship with food—to learn how to prepare it, eat it, and enjoy it responsibly. All of it.

At FP4H, we don't rule out any food groups.

Fad diets are fueled by our country's obsession with two diametrically-opposed concepts. We are obsessed with food, and we are obsessed with our appearance. We see commercials urging us to eat all we can, as much as we can, at every opportunity, yet the actors in the commercials wouldn't touch all that food they're supposedly eating. (Not if they wanted to work again!)

Every new diet always blames the food. We were told that the fat in food made us fat. Then all the world went sugar-free. According to Lisa Young, Ph.D. author of *The Portion Teller: Smartsize Your Way to Permanent Weight Loss*, neither carbs nor fats are the blame for America's obesity today. The blame belongs to the sheer volume. We are over-feeding our bodies, and it is not because we are physically hungry.

Being the national director of a faith-based weight loss program, people expect me to act like the food police. They assume I'm always looking at what they're eating and passing judgment. At lunch, my friend chooses to order french fries with her sandwich and says with a guilty look, "I know, I'm bad." I want to shake her and say that eating french fries can in no way make you a bad person.

Another friend sees me at the local deli and is quick to point out how "good" she is, as she lifts up her fresh veggie salad with no dressing. I want to tell her that eating those foods has nothing to do with whether or not she's a good person.

Food does not have the power to make us good or bad. It is not moral or immoral. In Jesus' day, the Jews struggled with this idea too. There were Pharisees who strictly followed not only the dietary restrictions God had given His people, but the hundreds of additional rules that teachers of the law had added. One day the Pharisees noticed that Jesus' disciples were eating food without performing all the customary ceremonial hand-washing rituals. These law-keepers thought that if you ate food with "unclean" hands, it would make the food "unclean" and make you "unclean" as well. God would see you as tainted, corrupted, or defiled.

Mark records Jesus' response.

> He answered, "Don't you know what I am talking about by now? You surely know that the

food you put into your mouth cannot make you unclean. It doesn't go into your heart, but into your stomach, and then out of your body." By saying this, Jesus meant that all foods were fit to eat (Mark 7:18-19).

The opposite is also true. If food cannot make me unclean, neither can it make me clean. In our minds, we have given food (or our food choices) the power to do something it cannot do—declare us good or bad, righteous or unrighteous. Jesus made us righteous with His death on the cross, when He paid the penalty for our sin, taking the punishment in our place.

At times, our food choices may be wise or unwise, healthy or unhealthy, better or worse. But they don't define us. They don't determine our value or worth. They don't make us bad or good. Food doesn't have that kind of power.

At FP4H, we want you to reach the place where you can enjoy—with freedom—every bite you eat, without fear, guilt, or shame. And may it be blessed in Jesus' name.

Food is Not the Enemy

The Live It Plan

The Live It Plan is not another deprivation diet that you won't be able to stick to, no matter how hard you try. The Live It Plan teaches you how to bring your weight to a healthy level by *choosing healthy foods in proper portions for your level of lifestyle activity*. That's it.

The First Place 4 Health nutrition plan is uncomplicated, straightforward, and good for life. Based on credible science and common sense, it provides 100-percent fad free, gimmick-less advice that will not only help you lose weight, but will also pave your way to better health. Most diets include the same principles over and over again, in new packaging—along with a few bogus claims made for marketing purposes. Despite all the hype, the bottom line is still the same: *calories in versus calories out*. However, we believe the calories you take in should be delicious, enjoyable, and contribute not only to weight maintenance but also to health enhancement. Remember, this is the *LIVE* It, not the *DIE* It plan!

The only catch is that you have to *do* it.

First Place 4 Health is *not* designed to teach you how to continue eating poorly while losing weight. It is a plan that will teach you to choose what is better for your health and your waistline, every day.

As defined by the *Dietary Guidelines for Americans 2011,* a healthy diet is one that "emphasizes fruits, vegetables, whole grains, and fat-free or low-fat milk and milk products; includes lean meats, poultry, fish, beans, eggs, and nuts; and is low in saturated fats, trans fats, cholesterol, salt (sodium), and added sugars."[7] That definition guides the First Place 4 Health Live It recommendations. We teach you how to eat these foods in moderate amounts, based on your daily caloric needs. I think you'll find our plan is practical, realistic, flexible, and delicious.

All food fits into one of three categories:

- Foods With Benefits
- Foods Without Benefits
- Foods With Detriments

Our desire is for you to choose the highest quality foods and eat those foods in proper quantities.

Food is Not the Enemy

Foods With Benefits

Foods with benefits provide a significant amount of the nutrients our bodies need for health and vitality.

It is permissible for me to choose to eat any foods, but I have decided I want to eat with a purpose. My purpose is better health. I want to live as long and as strong as I can. So as often as I can, I choose to eat foods with benefits.

My father died at the early age of 73 from heart disease. When my mother died at age 76, she had high blood pressure, diabetes, and lung cancer. I have the same DNA. It's been said that when you are born with this kind of genetic pre-disposition, it's like having a loaded gun placed at your head. When you choose to do nothing about it, it's like pulling the trigger.

I am faced with this choice every morning. We have homemade caramel cupcakes sitting on the counter—looking scrumptious. I could choose the cupcake for breakfast. It is permissible. (Remember, it would not make me a "bad" person, and no food is "off-limits" to me.) My usual breakfast is oatmeal—everyday oatmeal, oatmeal, oatmeal. I look at the cupcake. I weigh the possibilities: *oatmeal...cupcake...oatmeal.* Oatmeal lowers cholesterol and is high in fiber. I know I want foods with benefits, so I choose oatmeal, because I really want to keep my cholesterol in check. My eating has a purpose, and so can yours with the Live It Plan.

On a side note, the quality of food with benefits is relative, depending where you are on this wellness journey. For instance, generally speaking, choosing whole grain bread over white flour bread would be the quality choice. But for some people, packing a lunch with a sandwich on white bread instead of rushing through the drive-thru and ordering a high-fat, fast-food restaurant meal would be a quality decision. These are small manageable steps toward quality food. There is no condemnation in white bread or a supersized hamburger. The Apostle Paul wrote in 1 Corinthians 10:23 that "all things are permissible but not all things are beneficial." [*Paraphrase mine.*] You know what represents progress and positive change for you.

Foods With No Benefits

Foods with no benefits have no nutrients—they don't do anything for us. Choosing a nutrient-empty food is not sinful. It is permissible. I can choose to eat sugar free Jell-O for lunch. It has no fat or sugar, but it also has no benefits for me. It's a neutral food. Neither beneficial nor detrimental. There's nothing wrong with enjoying Jell-O, but we should ask ourselves if there is a "food with benefits" option I would enjoy just as much or more.

Foods With Detriments

Although in FP4H, we do not declare any foods "good" or "bad" or "off-limits," we recognize—and encourage you to recognize—that there are foods that can be detrimental to health if consumed on a regular basis. Many of these foods are overly processed, contain potentially harmful chemicals, or are dangerous to those with allergies, sensitivities, or certain diseases.

For example, my father suffered from gout in his later years. Every time he ate seafood, he experienced a painful flair-up with the gout and could barely walk. This choice of food was detrimental to his health and wellbeing. For others, seafood might be a good choice and have some excellent benefits. Those who suffer from celiac disease must avoid gluten, but others don't always benefit from eating "gluten-free."

This is why I love the Live It plan. I can personalize it for me. Your doctor can help you determine what is best for you to eat and what, if anything, you should avoid.

A Final Thought

Being a health and wellness professional, I personally prefer eat as "clean" as I can. I don't have celiac disease, but I did eat gluten-free for a year to fight some inflammation in my body. I avoid processed foods—foods that are loaded with chemicals—as much as possible. I have some specific convictions about this and some compelling reasons based on my family tree.

What represents "healthy food choices" for you—your list of "foods with benefits"—may be different than mine, or from others in your FP4H group, and that's okay. We're all on our own journey. As we ask God to guide us, He will help us find our way.

Chapter Five

Exercise Is Not a Dirty Word

The FP4H Live It plan is designed for healthy eating and moving your body. Studies show that losing weight is 70% what you eat and 30% what you do. It is true that you can lose weight without exercise, but who wouldn't want to lose 30% more? Not to mention all of the other benefits of exercise. When the FP4H program was updated in 2008, I wrote the exercise section of the materials. My research found 21 clinically proven benefits of exercise. There are now over 40. Exercise is the magic many of us have longed to find.

But I'm not going to lie; there is a problem with exercise: it can be painful, inconvenient, and downright hard work. And what's even worse, many of us think of exercise as punishment for our poor choices or our imperfect body. Making exercise a welcome part of a healthy lifestyle requires a complete paradigm shift in our thinking.

Let's deal with the issues first.

The Pain

Yes, it can be painful. But there is good pain and bad pain. We need to learn the difference. Whenever we start moving our body, there will be some aching and discomfort. Sore muscles are typical. Shortness of breath is common, when you increase the intensity of your workout. Unfortunately, most people quit when pain occurs. Exercise is hard work. *I think that why it's called a "workout."* It will be some of the hardest work you will ever do—but with lifelong benefits. Personally, I choose not to focus on the pain. I have osteoarthritis in both knees and polymyalgia rheumatica in my shoulder and hips. I still exercise every day. I refuse to focus on the pain; instead, I focus on the benefits. As long as I keep the knees moving, I am postponing a knee replacement. As long as I keep these shoulders rotating, I am preventing a frozen shoulder.

Ask yourself these questions: What can exercise give me? What does a new and healthy me look like one year from now? What will I be able to do that I cannot do now? Could I have enough energy to play with my kids or grandkids or finally go on that dream vacation or church missions trip?

Will I lower my insurance rates, because I can come off my medications? Will my back or knees stop hurting? Will my mood improve? Will I be able to sleep better at night?

These are good questions, but the most important one of all: "What blessing will I receive from the Lord for my obedience?"

We have much to do for the Kingdom and our bodies need to be strong. We cannot quit because of temporary discomfort. We can think and dream all day long about weighing less and being healthy. It's time to stop daydreaming, and put in the work to make it happen.

The Inconvenience

If it is important, you will find a way. If not, you will find an excuse.

There are a million and one excuses for why we can't find time to exercise, but we must rid ourselves of these pretexts. As my favorite biking tee shirt reads, "It's a hill, get over it."

I know you are busy. I am, too. I know it's not convenient to... go to the gym, dig out the exercise equipment, find a class, find a good video, find a workout buddy, find something to wear. It's not easy when you have small children or when you're a caregiver or when you work full-time or when you're confined to a wheelchair. But for every excuse, every problem, there is a solution. Someone somewhere has been in your shoes, and they found a way to make it work. You can too.

You can brainstorm ideas with your FP4H group. You can also go online and search for "ways to exercise with…" or "when…." Ask your friends to give you their favorite tips or recommend classes, videos, or scheduling tools, when you log on to your social media sites. You'll be amazed at what's available to you.

The bottom line: "You can have results or you can have your excuses. You cannot have both." – Unknown.

The Punishment

I no longer consider exercise punishment for the way I look—or as the penalty I pay for my poor choices. I consider my exercise an act of worship to my Lord.

Most of us think of worship as something we do on Sunday morning with friends and family, when the praise band is playing or we're sitting in a pew in a beautiful stained-glass building. As we exit the building, that's where our worship ends. Or does it?

In reality, many of us continue to worship, but at a different kind of altar. We head to the nearest all-you-can-eat buffet, giving praise to God, while we fill up our plates for a second and third time. Or we head home and collapse in the recliner, giving heed to almighty cable TV.

What if we could make a connection between our eating and exercise commitments and our worship? Earlier I described what it means to be a "living sacrifice." The Apostle Paul calls this our "spiritual act of worship" (Romans 12:1).

Our dedicated exercise time could actually become a holy encounter with the living God. The same is true when we choose not to eat unhealthy foods. God satisfies us above and beyond our physical appetites.

Presenting myself to God daily, in this body He has given me, has become a powerful discipline in my relationship with Him. An act of obedience, an act of sacrifice, an act of worship. It consecrates my day and my efforts to not only become healthy, but holy—set apart to glorify Him and not myself. I can't imagine living life any other way.

Chapter Six

Simple Steps to Get Started

Everyone I encounter on the health and wellness journey is somewhere on this timeline—either starting, starting over, or finishing. Regardless of where you are on the continuum, if you want to be successful, you must take action. Here are some simple steps to get you started:

Step One: Set Goals

Famous hockey player Wayne Gretzky once said, "You miss 100 percent of the shots you never take." We must have a plan. Setting goals is our first step. If we don't know where we want to go, how will we ever get there?

Since you are more than a one-sided person, you need more than a weight-loss goal. You need a goal in each area of your life: physical, emotional, mental, and spiritual.

Six Simple Steps to Get Started

Jesus was a goal setter.

The Bible says Jesus' goal was to reconcile us to God. From the beginning, it was His purpose to carry out the will of His Father. (See Luke 2:49 and John 4:34.)

> As the time drew near when Jesus would be taken up to heaven, he <u>made up his mind and set out on his way</u> to Jerusalem (Luke 9:51 GNB).

> And it came to pass, when the time was come that he should be received up, he steadfastly <u>set his face</u> to go to Jerusalem (Luke 9:51 KJV). [*Emphasis mine.*]

Set His face to go to Jerusalem? It is hard to imagine his determination because in that city, the cross awaited. Though Satan tried to tempt him to take a shortcut and to avoid the cross, He focused on His goal. Nothing could distract or stop Him.

He once explained to His disciples why He was more concerned about ministering to people than thinking about where He would get His next meal: "My food is to do the will of Him who sent me and to accomplish his work" (John 4:34 ESV).

The result of His unwavering focus and commitment was the redemption of all mankind.

Physical Goals

Your physicals goal will be the easiest to determine. For example, your goal may be to lose fifty pounds, lower your blood pressure, or increase your physical activity. These are important goals, and setting goals in every physical area will increase your chance of success in each one.

Emotional Goals

One of my emotional goals for this year is to develop a deeper relationship with my sister. We used to be close, but life circumstances, hurt feelings, and a lot of years rushing by have separated us. I desire for this relationship to be right and whole. It will take some effort on my part. Consider the relationships in your life. Is there a relationship that needs attention? Is there an issue in your heart that is unresolved? Could this unresolved issue be sabotaging your weight loss efforts? Make a goal to find a solution in some specific way.

Six Simple Steps to Get Started

Mental Goals

Keeping our minds fit and alert will help us stay focused on our other goals. A mental goal might be to challenge yourself to learn a new skill or take a class in (for example) a new language or computer proficiency. A mental goal I have set for myself is to become proficient in using my new Mac computer. Though definitely challenging, I am going to work hard to learn it well. I set a schedule to watch the tutorials, and I am developing new proficiencies and expertise.

Spiritual Goals

Consider setting a spiritual goal such as spending time with God each day or memorizing a chapter of Scripture. Perhaps your goal will be to develop a more consistent prayer life. I have set a spiritual goal to memorize one Bible verse a week for the rest of the year. It is helpful that my FP4H Bible study provides a Scripture a week for this purpose. Even though I have been in a class consistently for over twenty years, I have not always learned the Bible verses. This is a new goal for me. I know it will have a direct impact on my other goals.

A word about setting smart goals: I have been a goal-setter all of my life, but not always a goal achiever. Looking back, I think it is because I was not smart at setting goals. Setting smart goals will make a difference in your success. A guide to you set smart goals is found at the back of this book in the Appendix.

Step Two: Start with Small Steps, But Start

The next step to success is to make changes slowly, one at a time. You will get to your goal, if you do not give up. Consistency will bring results, but not if you get burned out or injured from the beginning. My getting-started philosophy is simply to avoid the "toos." Too much, too soon, too fast. It will take time to see results in your body, as well as your spirit. You didn't get out of shape overnight, so it is impractical to think you can change everything in less time.

Starting small is especially true in the area of exercise. Most of us begin with too much ambition, and then we overdo it. We don't take the proper precautions. We don't give our bodies enough time to make adjustments. The same excess happens when we take an "extreme" approach to the food we eat. Most of us have tried all of the crazy diets out there.

Six Simple Steps to Get Started

There are food plans that tell you not to eat anything but fruit and then maybe a few veggies. Some plans say avoid all meats or all grains. Others eliminate all sugars or all fats.

The problem with these food plans is they're too extreme and not sustainable. Making small changes in our eating habits will bring results over a period of time, and we won't get burned out on the food plan. I recall a funny incident where I didn't start small (at least, it's funny now). I had been on a diet that required me to avoid all grains, all sugar, and all fat. Sounds awful, doesn't it? It was! Rob, my husband, brought home a leftover box of donuts from the men's prayer breakfast. The second he set it on the counter I said, "Get out of my way. Don't try to stop me!" I dove for the box. I'm sure you can relate. Taking small steps will get you to your goal, one pound at a time, one step at a time.

Patience is indeed a virtue, and you will need it to make these changes, but the results may save your life. One of the top four reasons people give up on exercise is because they do not see the results quickly. James, the brother of Jesus, wrote to the church abroad: "Be patient, then, my friends, until the Lord comes. See how patient farmers are as they wait for their land to produce precious crops. They wait patiently for the autumn and spring rains" (James 5:7 GNB).

The same principle applies to exercise. If we are consistent and patient, our bodies and spirits will yield a valuable crop of wonderful fruit in the areas of heart health, weight loss, strength, and flexibility. We need to consistently sow in all of these areas of fitness so that in the end we will reap a harvest.

I'm so passionate about the benefits of exercise, I've written a book on it, *Don't Quit Get Fit*. For more information on this book and other resources go to the FP4H website www.firstplace4health.com.

Joyce Foreman has been in my FP4H class for almost four years. She'd tell you she's done "okay" without much exercise. But last year, she was finally convinced that she needed to add exercise to her life. She started coming to my Body & Soul Fitness class three times a week. Within six months, she was noticeably stronger—lifting heavy weights. But more important than the size of the weights, she was being consistent. Then last spring she suffered a stroke. Here are Joyce's words.

> With Vicki's encouragement and physician approval for moderate exercise, I began my exercise journey. I had been reluctant to join because of my age, thinking that I might be

the oldest person there (and I was), but I was never made to feel inadequate in any way. I was welcomed warmly and have managed to almost keep up. I was still struggling with jumping jacks and push-ups. Then I had a stroke. Because of the many prayers, special care of loving friends, wonderful medical attention, and the strength in my arms and legs, I was able to recover quickly. Exercise has helped me to prioritize my personal health by guarding my heart and adding a new dimension to my physical and spiritual wellbeing.

Yea, Joyce. I am so proud of her.

Research confirms that people who exercise recover more quickly from major episodes like strokes and heart attacks. In the July 2009 issue of the *Journal of Neurology, Neurosurgery & Psychiatry*, the researchers reported that stroke patients who had previously exercised regularly before a stroke occurred were significantly more likely to have milder impairments and were better able to care for themselves, compared to patients who rarely exercised. "It appears that exercise is beneficial to people at risk of developing a stroke," says Mayo Clinic neurologist James Meschia, M.D., the study's lead investigator. "Many studies have shown that exercise can reduce the risk of developing a stroke in the first place, and this study suggests that if an active person does have a stroke, outcomes can be improved."

Joyce's investment in exercise has made a huge difference in her life. She is back in my classes this fall, a wonderful example to the rest of us. Exercise pays off.

Even if we can't see immediate results, we must be patient and let God do His wonderful work in us.

Step Three: Adjust your Thinking

We've said it before: change that lasts a lifetime begins in the mind. Our thinking patterns have been ingrained in us since childhood. FP4H helps us develop skills to disrupt those life-long thought patterns—and develop new ones— through the power of the Holy Spirit. No more toxic thinking. We now set our minds on the same things the Spirit has for us.

> For those who live according to the flesh set their minds on the things of the flesh, but those who live according to the Spirit set their minds on the things of the Spirit (Romans 8: 5 ESV).

Six Simple Steps to Get Started

This verse says that a willful, purposeful, deliberate decision helps us think the way we want to think. It is a recalibration of the mind, which moves us in a new direction.

I use the GPS on my phone to get me where I'm going. I can easily take a wrong turn, especially if I think I know better than the map. My GPS helps me recalibrate and then drive in the right direction. Wellness also requires us to make some major adjustments in the way we think.

Adjusting our thinking means focusing on positive changes beyond weight loss. Making better choices as we commit to healthy eating, getting regular exercise, discovering the meaning of true self-esteem and self-acceptance. All of these objectives are part of a holistic approach to health. Strength and health have less to do with a number on a scale than the ability to balance and nurture all aspects of life—the emotional, mental, and spiritual, as well as the physical.

Here are some examples of common thought patterns—misconceptions—that might need adjustment.

- **Common thinking.** Starving myself is the best way to lose weight.

- **Adjusted thinking.** Healthy, relaxed eating in response to being hungry is key to maintaining a comfortable relationship with food and to avoid over feeding my body.

- **Common thinking.** People need to be thin in order to be healthy and happy.

- **Adjusted thinking.** People have a wide variety of God-given body shapes and sizes. We all need to accept and be grateful that we are fearfully and wonderfully made by our Creator.

Wayne Ellis

I used to be so skinny as a kid that I prayed to gain weight. Well, God waited until I hit middle age to answer that prayer. The stretch of life when I needed to be lean and keen, I wasn't. I was overweight and gaining about 10 pounds every two years. About the time I became a senior citizen, I weighed 280 lbs. Now the weight hung around me like a death sentence. I knew I needed to do something, but I had very little will or motivation and even less information to get it done.

Six Simple Steps to Get Started

We began First Place 4 Health in our church, and I signed up. I have to say I was skeptical about it, personally. I knew that intense exercise was out for me, because of some physical limitations, and I knew that my will power was not too strong either. If you are looking for an excuse, I am the type of guy who can help you find one. I was perfect for failure.

The FP4H program gave me the tools I needed to change my mind, my diet, and my lifestyle. The information about eating what is good for the body instead of what is quick, easy, and full of sugar was the message that I needed to hear. I discovered I was actually living from sugar rush to sugar rush. I didn't think getting off that roller coaster was going to be easy, but I was surprised. A healthy diet was what my body was waiting for.

Everybody has to count something, so I only counted calories. I kept breakfast and lunch to around 700 or 800 calories and no more than 1000 calories for supper and a snack. I was losing weight on 1800-2000 calories per day. Those numbers show how much I was previously taking in. Then I discovered that I could actually drop the calorie count to 1500 without too much difficulty and did so on occasion.

The weight did not roll off, but a pound or two pounds per week was like victory upon victory. I had some weeks without weight loss, but no gains either, and the following week I might drop 3-5 pounds. I learned not to reward myself with food. I found that intentionally spending time and deep personal conversation with others was like a balm to my spirit and an encouragement to my soul.

I cannot say enough for the spiritual content that First Place 4 Health naturally leads a person to discover. The fellowship with other folks who struggle with weight and want better things physically and spiritually is such an encouragement and support in the sessions. The Bible studies, testimonies, and the focus in God's Word help to put everything together. It is amazing how the spiritual and the physical affect and connect with each other. Men, FP4H is a journey you will not be sorry to have taken.

Six Simple Steps to Get Started

Adjusting your thinking will take a great deal of work on your part. Do not be surprised if it takes time—you will not beat the enemy overnight. It took me years to erase the tapes of lies and deceit that constantly played over and over in my mind. But those images of habits and episodes that dishonored God, and those words of defeat that I heard spoken over me no longer have power over me. I can barely see or remember the lies anymore. They have been replaced with the glorious truth of God's Word and the heavenly images of experiences and memories of the things I now participate in that bring glory to God.

We are not hopelessly unable to change. He can do a mighty work—if we are willing to submit ourselves to Him, and do our part to participate in the process.

Chapter Seven

Counting the Cost

Make no mistake: Getting healthy physically, spiritually, mentally, and emotionally will be the hardest work you have ever done. It will be costly.

It will cost money. Good food is not cheap, and neither are the good tools and resources that will help you along the way.

It will cost time and energy. For instance, planning for healthy meals and making time for exercise will be an adjustment. Taking the time to write down your food after every meal is time-consuming. You may have to shut the computer down an hour earlier, so you can get the sleep you need to get up and make it to an exercise class. You may have to expend extra energy, working up a sweat.

You may find you have to give up some things you've enjoyed in the past, because they aren't helping you move forward and into your future. And although you will have a built-in accountability and support group with FP4H, you may find not all of your friends and family are as anxious to help you make significant life changes.

It isn't easy to give God first place, to offer ourselves to Him as living sacrifices.

The Old Testament records the story of King David and Araunah. David knew he had brought a plague upon Israel through his own sinful actions. He repented and begged God for mercy.

> Then the angel of the LORD ordered Gad to tell David to go up and build an altar to the LORD on the threshing floor of Araunah the Jebusite. So David went up in obedience to the word that Gad had spoken in the name of the LORD. While Araunah was threshing wheat, he turned and saw the angel; his four sons who were with him hid themselves.

> Then David approached, and when Araunah looked and saw him, he left the threshing floor and bowed down before David with his face to the ground.

David said to him, "Let me have the site of your threshing floor so I can build an altar to the LORD, that the plague on the people may be stopped. Sell it to me at the full price."

Araunah said to David, "Take it! Let my lord the King do whatever pleases him. Look, I will give the oxen for the burnt offerings, the threshing sledges for the wood, and the wheat for the grain offering. I will give all this."

But King David replied to Araunah, "No, I insist on paying the full price. I will not take for the LORD what is yours, or sacrifice a burnt offering that costs me nothing" (1 Chronicles 21:18-24).

David knew the value of sacrifice. Because it cost something, he also discovered that experiencing the temporary pain of sacrifice opens the door to tremendous blessing. Sacrifice is worship. Amazing things happen when we're willing to say, "God, I want you more than anything else. I want You *first.*"

From now on, consider each time you give up sleep and get out of bed to meet with Him as an act of worship. Every

Counting the Cost

time you use the stairs instead of the elevator is an act of worship. When you pick up your running shoes instead of watching TV and when you choose to engage your body in exercise, it is an act of worship and a costly sacrifice.

As a high school senior in Jacksonville, Florida, I was introduced to an organization called the Fellowship of Christian Athletes (FCA). We met monthly to hear an inspirational speaker and discuss the challenges of living for Christ, on and off the field. Years later, I decided to help the FCA chapter at my kids' high school. In reviewing the materials, I came across the FCA creed. I think there are some ideas in this creed that we, adult athletes, who are pursuing wellness, should consider embracing. I'm quoting part here, with permission.

My body is the temple of Jesus Christ.
I protect it from within and without.
Nothing enters my body that
does not honor the living God.
My sweat is an offering to my Master.
My soreness is a sacrifice to my Savior.
I give my all—all of the time.
I do not give up. I do not give in.
I do not give out. I am the Lord's warrior -
a competitor by conviction

and a disciple of determination.
I am confident beyond reason
because my confidence lies in Christ.
The results of my efforts
must result in His glory.
My sweat is an offering to my Master.
My soreness is a sacrifice to my Savior.

Let those words sink in for a minute. This idea of offering and sacrifice is the final motivation we have been looking for. Our sweat and our soreness and our effort are making the sacrifice, because we love our Savior, and we are devoted to Him. At the end of my boot camp classes, we huddle up, pray, and then wipe our brows and hold out our sweat offering for the Lord. We pray that He will find it acceptable and pleasing, because we have made the sacrifice. Our sweat is our offering.

P. J. Bahr

All of my childhood, I was called "Patty." Well, we all know what rhymes with that name— "fatty." Psychologists say that children become what is spoken to them and over them. I grew to live up to the wretched nickname, "Fatty Patty."

Counting the Cost

Someone suggested that I write my name with an "i" at the end instead of a "y," so I started spelling my name "Patti." It looked "thinner." Unfortunately, I wasn't thin, so I went from diet plan to diet plan and diet pill to diet pill.

Having grown up with an alcoholic father and a verbally abusive big brother, I heard often that because of my obesity and appearance, I shouldn't go out in public. I was told it was a disservice to the community for them to have to gaze on my appearance. I would never amount to anything nor find a man to marry me.

In my twenties, I married an alcoholic and had two small children. I had eaten my way to about 340 pounds and was absolutely miserable. My husband left our children and me for a young, vivacious 18-year-old girl. The words I heard growing up echoed constantly in my mind, and I became a recluse.

My husband wasn't contributing financially to our household any longer, so I had to do anything I could to support our two little children and myself. The city where I lived posted a job that required working only at night, the city janitor. I applied and got the job. I thought I'd be safe at night when I didn't have to see people—or rather, be seen.

Each night I loaded my two little kids in my old blue Plymouth Volare station wagon, along with industrial cleaning equipment, vacuums, shampooers, chemicals, and we cleaned the Library, City Hall, and City Auditorium. Sturgis, South Dakota, and the Sturgis City Auditorium is home to the world's largest motorcycle rally every August, and I can't describe the filth and grime we had to clean. When I'd go to clean City Hall, occasionally the commissioners or council people would be leaving a meeting as I was arriving, and the stares I got are vivid in my mind—after 30 years.

After daily pleading, begging, crying, and more begging for my husband to return to us proved futile, I met with a Christian counselor. Then a cousin who passionately loved Jesus wanted to do anything to help me.

Slowly, I began to study the Bible, lose weight, and come out of my shell.

Counting the Cost

I took a different job, a nights-only job as a 911 operator for the local police department and sheriff's office. There I met a policeman whose wife was a bodybuilder. They worked out a few times a week at a free gym, and asked me to join them. I started going with them. One time they pulled up in my driveway, and I said that I didn't feel like going that night. They said they were going to sit in the driveway until I came outside. About 20 minutes later, I relented and got in their car. They were so incredibly motivating and kind to me. When I was sweating profusely at the gym, they would say, "Come on Patti, you can play another 5 minutes of basketball. One day you'll have the guys lined up on your front porch." I thought they were absolutely insane, but I'd play another five minutes.

After several months, I transferred to Rapid City where I met my current husband. We dated almost three years before I found the courage to tell him I had been terribly obese. I had to know I could really trust him to not reject me, before I could share my dark secret with him. I didn't show him the one "before" picture I had saved, until a couple years later when we were married.

I had destroyed any pictures of myself in my "wretched" state, so to this day, I only have one photograph.

After Don and I had been married about five years, my weight began creeping up again. Knowing my propensity to easily weigh over 300 pounds, I began to panic. But I knew I had no success with diet programs. Prayerfully, I sought the Lord on almost a moment-by-moment basis. The fear was debilitating to me.

One Saturday, my husband asked me to join him as he went on his occasional "gold prospecting" venture. Desiring to be a good wife, I said I would go, but asked if I could stop at the local Christian bookstore and buy a book to take along. We stopped at the store and I prayed and asked the Lord to lead me to a book that would help me deal with this issue of weight.

On a shelf of thin paperbacks, I found a book talking about giving Christ first place in your life. First place over anything—including your appetite. I devoured every page of the book and found the website for First Place 4 Health on the back cover. That was in the late fall of the year 2000.

Like an alcoholic who never says, "I've licked my drinking problem and it's no longer a concern," I never say, "I've gotten to my goal weight and now I can eat whatever I want, whenever I want." Maintaining my weight and my health is not only daily, but also moment-by-moment, relying on the Lord to keep my focus in proper perspective.

First Place 4 Health and Your Community

When I started my first FP4H group, I had no idea the impact it would have on me personally and my church and community.

Until the fall of 1993, I had been able to stay in pretty good shape. Not perfect, but good enough. But in 1993, I had what I call my personal four-sided person train wreck. I told myself I already knew how to get in shape, and I needed to simply buckle down and do it.

One day, three significant situations converged that helped me begin my amazing journey.

First, my fourth child was almost one-year-old. While this child was a pleasant surprise, he was still a surprise! I managed my eating and exercise pretty well at first, but eventually it was all I could do to get out of bed and care for my four children, much less exercise. That led to the second significant situation: I gained quite a bit of weight. Soon I weighed more than I had ever weighed. I could no longer pretend not to care. I had to deal with the issue of weight and how to lose it. After my previous pregnancies, I had managed to eventually lose the extra pounds, but this time was different. I don't know if it was my age or a lack of time and motivation. Around this time, we bought our first Internet-ready computer, which was the third significant situation. Sitting at our new computer, I experienced a life-changing crisis.

As I booted up the computer for the first time, it asked me to create a password. I needed something I would not forget, something that I thought about every day. The perfect password came way too quickly—I thought about my weight every day. Discouraged and feeling hopeless about the size of my body, I had become convinced that I would never lose the weight.

Counting the Cost

As I sat at my computer, the password came to me in the form of a prayer: *Lord, is there any hope for me to lose this weight? Can you help me? Can you help me help myself?* In my mind, I knew what I needed to do to lose the weight, but the feeling of hopelessness was overwhelming. My new password, "hope 4 me," became my prayer every day.

About the same time, my mother-in-law, Lou Heath, saw my struggle and mentioned a new weight loss group called First Place, which was meeting at her church in Nashville. "It's like Weight Watchers for Christians," she encouraged. First Place was hosting a training meeting in Ocala, Florida, and a glimmer of hope was born in my heart.

I called Melanie, a friend who knew and understood my struggle, to ask if she was interested in taking a road trip with me to learn about this new Christian way of weight loss. Since she was struggling too, she said yes. When we arrived at the training, I noticed that the other hundred or so attendees seemed to be in the same shape as me. I was encouraged immediately. Several people shared testimonies of how First Place had been a Godsend in their lives. When climbed on the scale, I said to myself, *I never have to weigh this again.* It's now seventeen years later, and I haven't.

Back home, we enlisted a small group of women who shared our weight problems and frustrations. I made them swear an oath that we would tell no one what we were doing—in case of failure. What little faith I had. Failure had become an old familiar friend, and I did not want to renew the relationship again. We met in secret on Sunday nights, and despite my lack of faith, we all experienced success. And it was obvious. One friend lost 80 pounds in a year. This created a firestorm of curiosity in our church and community. We grew to five groups. We had men-only groups, early-morning groups, and co-ed groups. Our church became known as the church that cares about the whole person. Many came to Christ through these years, including Terri.

Terri Putman Ledford

God was not new to me. I was raised in the Methodist Church. But somehow I missed the part about Jesus being my "personal" Savior. By my mid-thirties, my life was dark and hopeless. When I graduated from high school, I moved out on my own ready to conquer the world— instead the world conquered me. I stopped going to church and began a long string of poor decisions, based on living in the moment. I got married and divorced, had a child born out of wedlock, and subsequently married the father of my son. It was not long into the marriage when

Counting the Cost

I realized that my spouse had a serious drug and alcohol addiction.

I was no innocent bystander in the beginning, but my situation progressively became worse. My spouse became verbally and physically abusive, and as is common in families with drug and alcohol addicts, my self-esteem eroded. I began to gain weight and lose hope.

I enrolled my 2-year-old son into daycare at Remount Road Baptist Church. I noticed a flyer on the door of the daycare for a Body & Soul aerobic class being offered on Monday and Thursday nights, and I decided to check it out. I made arrangements and showed up for the first class. The class was a blast, and I kept coming back. I developed friendships with the women in the class and joined them at church on Sunday and eventually Sunday Bible study. I saw joy, love, and light in the faces and lives of these women—and I wanted what they had.

I mentioned that I was raised in the Methodist church. Now I was attending a Baptist church. I felt God calling me to trust Him, yet every time

I tried to take a step out of my row to go to the front of the church in response to the invitation, I could not do it. My feet were firmly planted in the back row. So I prayed silently and agreed to trust God. From this moment, my life changed, and I was filled with joy and hope for the first time in a long time.

Later I shared the news with my pastor and his wife (who was the aerobics instructor) and requested to be baptized. I thought I could work around that going-to-the-front-of-the-church routine. Pastor Heath said, "Great. Next Sunday during the invitation, come on down, and we will make the proclamation to the church family together." God does have a sense of humor.

I joined the church and my faith began to grow. My church started the First Place 4 Health program, and I was quick to sign up. I lost 40 pounds and gained joy, peace, and hope. My faith in God continues to grow today, and as I look back on my transformation from darkness to light, I can testify that we can overcome every situation with God—if we give Him control.

Counting the Cost

Not only did our church grow, but many of the churches in our community grew also. Those who came to our classes were encouraged to go back and start new classes in their churches. To be a part of this growth was a wonderful personal faith experience for me.

The Wellness Journey of a Lifetime

Terri Putman Ledford

Counting the Cost

The opportunities to share your faith in FP4H are limitless. I remember two women who came to my class from different faith backgrounds. They were not familiar with Bible study or prayer. They asked for help in purchasing their first Bibles. How exciting to see God's Word come alive for them week after week. And the prayer time! On one occasion, as I closed in prayer, I prayed for one of these gals by name. As class members began to leave the room, I noticed that she remained seated and was openly weeping. I immediately asked if something was the matter.

"No," she said, "It's just that I have never heard anyone call out my name to God before."

I will never forget the impact of her statement. There are those in our communities who desperately need what Christ has to offer, and they will find it through FP4H. Your participation can not only help you, but it may also be a way for you to reach out and encourage others.

P. J. Bahr

Once I offered a FP4H class at another church in our city, and 65 people signed up. On the first night, one lady said, "You mean this is a class on weight loss. Good grief. I thought it was a regular Bible study. I don't want to do this. Sure I'm overweight, but my entire family is overweight. We're all big-boned; this is the way we are."

A couple weeks later, I encouraged members to write in their prayer journals at least once a day. I suggested they could begin with only one line, thanking God for something that day, or if they felt overwhelmed, they could simply write, "Dear Lord. I'm too busy."

This same lady announced in front of the class, "No way! I am not going to do that. I am much too busy. I'm a single mom and I work full-time. There's no way I have time to write in a journal."

I gently encouraged her to pray and give it a try.

Several weeks later, she told the class that she couldn't live without her prayer journal. "The journal writing keeps me from overeating in the evenings, because I write in it rather than snack." This same woman began to lose weight and eventually dropped from size 20 to a size 8.

Counting the Cost

There was another woman who came in on the first night, and after learning the class was a Bible study, groaned, rolled her eyes, and chose to sit outside the room in the hallway, (but within listening distance) while staring at the wall clock. Her attitude was less than pleasant that night, and I never thought she'd stick with it. Well she did. At week three, I requested someone volunteer to be the group "encourager," and send a one-line email to each member. Guess who volunteered for that task?

The studies I led were not limited to women. A few men signed up, most with their wives. One man was terribly quiet, introverted, and never said a word, but he completed his weekly tracker and Bible study each week. At the end of the session, I asked if anyone would be interested in leading a study the next session, and shyly he said he thought he could handle it. He led a group with great success.

Today he is outgoing—and thinner—and quick to share that his physician discontinued his blood pressure medications.

Not only did I personally witness a miraculous transformation in my life through FP4H, I also witnessed miraculous transformations in the lives of others.

We join FP4H to lose weight, but we discover how to focus on growing in Christ and learning to give Him "first place," rather than losing weight, which is why, 14 years later, I'm still committed to FP4H on a daily basis. I need it. And I need each member who signs up. If others didn't participate, I would be alone on this path, and I love how God brings others to link arms with us as we stumble along.

Final Step: Trust Him

All of these steps are impossible without the power of God. We can follow these recommendations for a while, but most of us give up. We think it's too hard or too painful, and then when whatever reason or excuse comes along, most of us quit.

The reality: God in us is the only hope for change. He has the power to accomplish all that we have started. (See Colossians 1:27b.)

Counting the Cost

Trust Him to do what only He can do—to transform you completely and make you new. He will help you do all of the hard work to bring health to your body and your spirit. You must take the first step. As Becky Turner says, "You want to walk on water? You have to get out of the boat."

Jesus is here to help you. He has the power to help you lose weight. He has the power to heal you of your diseases. He has the power to help, and He will if you ask Him.

> Then they came to Jericho. As Jesus and his disciples, together with a large crowd, were leaving the city, a blind man, Bartimaeus (that is, the Son of Timaeus), was sitting by the roadside begging.
>
> When he heard that it was Jesus of Nazareth, he began to shout, "Jesus, Son of David, have mercy on me!"
>
> Many rebuked him and told him to be quiet, but he shouted all the more, "Son of David, have mercy on me!"
>
> Jesus stopped and said, "Call him." So they called to the blind man, "Cheer up! On your feet! He's calling you."

> Throwing his cloak aside, he jumped to his feet and came to Jesus. "What do you want me to do for you?" (Mark 10:46-51)

On that day, Jesus asked the question, and the blind man responded, "Rabbi, I want to see."

The blind man's answer was clear and specific and honest. And he received what he asked for.

> "Go," said Jesus, "your faith has healed you." Immediately he received his sight and followed Jesus along the road (Mark 10:52).

I believe Jesus is asking you the same question. "What do you want me to do for you?"

How will you answer Him? What do you want Him to do? Whatever it is, He can.

He will.

And when you're ready to take your first step here at First Place 4 Health, we're ready and willing to help you.

About the Author

Vicki Heath is national director and CEO of First Place 4 Health, a faith-based wellness ministry. She is a faculty member and certified instructor for the American Council on Exercise and a Bible teacher. Vicki is passionate about Christ and has a desire  to help others understand the value of caring for their spirits—as well as their bodies. Vicki teaches powerfully on total-person wellness—body, soul, mind, and spirit—from a biblical perspective. Vicki's classes are always fun, motivating, and doctrinally sound. She is the author of *Don't Quit Get Fit* (Regal Books) and writing contributor for First Place 4 Health curriculum. Vicki is a pastor's wife, mother of four, and grandmother of five. She lives on Edisto Island, South Carolina.

Appendix 1

How to Begin Your FP4H Journey

How to Start a Group

As a First Place 4 Health leader, you have the awesome privilege to witness lives radically changed as your members learn what it means to give Christ first place emotionally, spiritually, mentally, and physically. Your class members will lose weight and learn how to exercise, but the deepest life change can occur when Jesus Christ becomes Lord in their lives.

To begin your program, follow these easy steps:

1. Identify a location for your group meetings.

Enthusiasm is the primary qualification for becoming a First Place 4 Health group leader. While leaders are not required to be at their goal weight before leading a class, they should be following the program and moving toward their goal weight as an example to the group.

Many First Place 4 Health programs are hosted by a church. If your church does not have a group, ask your pastor or another local pastor about sponsoring the First Place 4 Health program. Communicate that the First Place 4 Health program is a biblically based and medically trustworthy wellness program. It can be used as an outreach tool and a ministry of discipleship. Programs can be scheduled in four 12-week sessions, with weekly meetings of one hour and 15 minutes.

Meetings can also be held in homes, neighborhood centers, campuses, hospitals, or the workplace. Be sure to discuss possible meeting days and times, requirements and expectations for proper care of the facilities, and the availability and cost of childcare.

Give them time to review your proposal and information. (Don't forget to pray.) And then follow up. When you receive approval, it's time to become familiar with the First Place 4 Health Group Starter Kit.

2. Purchase the First Place 4 Health leader materials.

To begin a First Place 4 Health group, you will need to purchase a First Place 4 Health Group Starter Kit. It contains everything you need to start a group. The Leader's Guide is an essential reference guide that contains practical and easy-to-follow instructions for how to set up the program, how to recruit and train leaders, how to conduct weekly meetings, how to plan a victory celebration, and much more. Also included are lesson plans, document samples, and reproducible forms.

The Bible study *Seek God First* is included in the Group Starter Kit. Use it for your first 12-week session. For future sessions the leader chooses a new Bible study for the group. See the complete list of available Bible studies on the First Place 4 Health website. The DVD, *Why Should a Christian Be Physically Fit?* by Dr. Richard Couey explains how eating the proper nutrients can help prevent disease. *Simple Ideas for Health Living* contains health tips and information on a wide range of topics that leaders can use as part of the wellness spotlight in each week's meeting. View all the items in the Group Starter Kit in the online store at www.FirstPlace4Health.com.

3. Publicize and promote your group.

Once you know the where and when of your First Place 4 Health group(s) and have scheduled your orientation, you can begin publicizing your group. Get creative! *The Leader's Guide* is full of tips on how to get the word out. Then register your group on the First Place 4 Health website.

4. Ask members to purchase the necessary materials.

When you have a leader and a group of individuals interested in starting the program, each new member will need a First Place 4 Health Member's Kit and a Bible study. The Member's Kit is a one-time purchase and contains everything the individual members in your group need to succeed. Each returning member needs only the First Place 4 Health Bible study selected for the upcoming session.

5. Determine if additional fees are required.

When more funds are needed to cover start-up expenses —a reliable scale for weekly weigh ins, leader materials, incentive awards, victory celebrations, leadership training, tape measures—it becomes necessary to charge individuals an additional registration fee, usually $10-$20. Some groups may want to consider adding childcare and scholarship costs to their fees as well. First Place 4 Health advises leaders to consult with their pastor or other church official to determine the registration fee to be collected from each member or couple.

6. Encourage members to read the First Place 4 Health Newsletter.

To enhance the success of each member's First Place 4 Health experience, leaders should encourage members to subscribe to the First Place 4 Health Newsletter. This valuable online resource supplements learning, provides new recipes, and inspires members to keep Christ in first place.

Appendix 2

How to Set a Smart Goal

Use this tool to help you set smart goals in all four areas of your life—physical, mental, emotional, and spiritual. Smart goals are

Specific. Be precise and detailed as you describe your goal. For example: *I want to grow in my walk with the Lord this year* is a worthy goal, but it is vague and broad. Instead, identify exactly what you want to accomplish.

- I will memorize one verse each week.
- I will practice faithfulness by attending church each week.
- I will become a regular tither.

Measurable. Set a goal that can be measured.

- I will enter my food in the food tracker each day.
- I will take my body measurements at the end of six weeks.
- I will read the FP4H Members Guide.

Action-Oriented. Decide what to do.

- I will set my alarm and exercise for at least 10 minutes every morning
- I will go to bed 30 minutes earlier.
- I will cook supper ahead of time twice this week.

Realistic. Determine if my goal is achievable based on my history, lifestyle, or present circumstances. Be ambitious, but not ridiculous.

- I will memorize one chapter from a New Testament book.
- I will lose an average of 1 pound each week for 12 weeks.
- I will avoid fried foods.

Trusted. There must be a faith element to all of our goals. "Only the weak attempt to accomplish what he knows he can already achieve." – Stella Juarez

- I will ask God to help me keep a journal each day.
- I will depend on God to break my addiction to sugar by asking Him to remind me when I am tempted.
- I will make a list of verses that declare God's love for me.

End Notes

1 http://www.cdc.gov/PDF/Facts_About_Obesity_in_
the_United_States.pdf)

2 http://www.usda.gov/factbook/chapter2.pdf

3 http://www.cdc.gov/diabetes/statistics/prev/national/
figpersons.htm

4 Obesity and Sleep; National Sleep Foundation.
Obesity hypoventilation syndrome (OHS); MedlinePlus.
Obesity and Cancer Risk; National Cancer Institute.

5 Author's notes from FP4H Wellness Week, Round Top
Texas, October 2014.

6 It's important to understand that the Bible is not against
pleasure—even pleasure that comes from eating. The
danger comes with greed. According to some studies, the
average American overfeeds his body by 30%.

7 U.S. Department of Health and Human Services and
U.S. Department of Agriculture, *Dietary Guidelines
for Americans, 2011,* 6th ed. (Washington, DC: U.S.
Government Printing Office, January 2005).

Bible Translations and Versions used in
The Wellness Journey of a Lifetime

Unless otherwise marked, Scripture quotations are taken from the Holy Bible, New International Version®, NIV®. Copyright © 1973, 1978, 1984, 2011 by Biblica, Inc.™ Used by permission of Zondervan. All rights reserved worldwide. www.zondervan. com The "NIV" and "New International Version" are trademarks registered in the United States Patent and Trademark Office by Biblica, Inc.™

Scripture quotations marked THE MESSAGE are taken from THE MESSAGE, copyright© by Eugene H. Person 1993, 1994, 1995, 1996, 2000, 2001, 2002. Used by permission of NavPress Publishing Group.

Scriptures marked GNB are quoted are from the Good News Bible © 1994 published by the Bible Societies/HarperCollins Publishers Ltd UK, Good News Bible© American Bible Society 1966, 1971, 1976, 1992. Used with permission.

Scripture quotations marked CEV are from the Contemporary English Version Copyright © 1991, 1992, 1995 by American Bible Society, Used by Permission.

Scripture quotations marked BBE are from The Bible in Basic English. Public domain. 1941, 1949, 1960, 1965.

4 first place 4health

discover a new way to healthy living

First Place 4 Health is the Christ-centered program that will help people lose weight and gain an all-new healthy lifestyle, while building a supportive network of friends. Proven and effective, **First Place 4 Health** will transform your life in every way—physically, mentally, spiritually and emotionally. Now's the time to join!

GROUP STARTER KIT CONTAINS:
- A Complete Member's Kit
- First Place 4 Health Leader's Guide
- Seek God First Bible Study
- First Place 4 Health Orientation and Food Plan DVD
- How to Lead with Excellence DVD
- 25 brochures on the First Place 4 Health program
- FP4H Canvas Tote Bag

MEMBER'S KIT CONTAINS:
- The Wellness Journey of a Lifetime Book
- First Place 4 Health Member's Guide
- Simple Ideas for Healthy Living
- Why Should a Christian Be Physically Fit? DVD
- Emotions & Eating DVD
- First Place 4 Health Prayer Journal

"A life-changing program with biblical integrity."
BETH MOORE
Best-selling author

Available at www.firstplace4health.com or by calling 1-800-727-5223.